Minding Your Own Business

Minding Your Own Business

Jim Green

Copyright Jim Green 2007
All Rights Reserved.

Printing: April. 2007

Published in the USA by
Profits Publishing of Sarasota, Florida
http://profitspublishing.com

Table of Contents

Preface 11
Prologue 13

Part 1 - Tackling the Deadly Mistakes Head On 17

1. **Broadening your horizons generates new ideas** 19
   Broadening horizons within your own area of expertise
   Tapping into your innate fountain of new ideas
   When you come up with an idea
   Factual experience
   Helpful hint

2. **Nurturing the plan that never stops evolving** 25
   Your plan starts and ends with you
   Where to begin
   Slotting in the nuts and bolts
   Factual experience
   Helpful hint

3. **Moving with the times stops you lagging behind** 31
   Keeping an open eye on the competition
   Keeping pace with the cyberspace opportunity
   Making the Internet work for you
   The value of a good web site
   Factual experience
   Helpful hint

4. **Control the cash or risk certain closure** 39
   Why cash is king
   Why you must keep a cash book
   Structuring your cash flow to best effect
   Paying your way
   Collecting dues
   Why till dipping is a no-no

Never try to trade you way out of trouble
Factual experience
Helpful hint

5. Keeping good employees and promoting from within ... 45
Getting good staff in the first place
Creative ways to reward your employees
Imparting your wisdom to help them grow
When good employees outgrow their positions
Cutting loose the deadwood
Helping employees to move on
Promoting from within
Factual experience
Helpful hint

6. Living in the real world in two minds 51
Operating on the left-hand side of the brain
Operating on the right-hand channel
Confusing likelihood with reality
Striking a balance between the thought processes
Becoming centred and single-minded in decision making
Factual experience
Helpful hint

7. There's no sale until the cash is in the bank 57
Determining your pricing strategy
Forecasting and targeting sales
Appreciating the nature of your sales machine
Why there is no sale until you collect your dues
Factual experience
Helpful hint

8. You cannot prosper doing it all by yourself 61
Yes, you can delegate
Delegation allows you to expand your own capabilities
Factual experience
Helpful hint

9. Cashing in on someone else's grey hairs 65
What to look for in selecting a part-time 'mastermind'
Where you find an elder statesperson
How much should you expect to pay?
Factual experience
Helpful hint

10. Pick yourself up and start all over again 69
Proper planning is the key
Why you should never consider giving up
Factual experience
Helpful hint

Part 2 - Maintaining Progress with Mastermind Strategies 73

11. Actualising self-confidence breaks down barriers 75
Assumptions have an influence on self-confidence
The danger of self-defeating thought patterns
Strategies for developing self-confidence
Factual experience
Helpful hint

12. Decisiveness: the key to achievement 83
When instant decisions are required
How to handle the introspection process
How to proceed decisively
Factual experience
Helpful hint

13. Devising a strategy for every situation 89
Why most start-ups flounder and go under
Everyday strategies for personal development
Strategic planning for opportunity
Factual experience
Helpful hint

14. Mastering the art of providing good service 97
Avenue of opportunity
Eight secrets for successful e-service
Survey your web site visitors
Factual experience
Helpful hint

15 The amazing power of words in minding your own business 105
Putting the magic of words to work in your business
Factual experience
Helpful hint

16. Developing your own distinctive style 113
How two brothers revolutionised an entire industry
Creating your own distinctive style

Factual experience
Helpful hint

17. Getting what you want with gentle persuasion 119
Selling the future
How do you do that?
Persuasion as a selling tool
Is selling a talent, a skill, or a process?
Factual experience
Helpful hint

18. Prepare to persist in your quest for achievement 125
They finally listened to the voice of persistence
Persisting to achieve
Factual experience
Helpful hint

19. Appreciating the awesome effect of humility 131
Skills based on qualities you already possess
Factual experience
Helpful hint

20. How to handle unreliable people 137
Why it always pays to insist on total reliability
Why you must never condone unreliability
Factual experience
Helpful hint

21. How to react to pressurised situations 141
We all get the same 24 hours
Addressing the 'It's required yesterday' syndrome
Staunching pressure before it reaches boiling point
Factual experience
Helpful hint

22. How to cope with treachery 147
Treachery within your own ranks
Treachery from a customer
Treachery from a supplier
Treachery from a competitor
Coping with acts of betrayal
Factual experience
Helpful hint

23. Facing up to the fear factor 153
The positive side of fear

Some matters of concern for small business operators
Addressing problematic situations as they occur
How to handle the fear factor
Factual experience
Helpful hint

24. How to manage in a crisis 159
Examples of crises that can strike any business at any time
Factual experience
Helpful hint

25. Cultivate intuition by listening to the inner voice 167
Slowing down and listening to the inner voice
How attuned are you to the subtle messages around you?
Soften your awareness
Try this simple exercise
Factual experience
Helpful hint

26. Learning to ask for what you want 173
Who can you ask for what you want?
How do you go about asking?
When did you last ask your employees for information?
Could you include a win-win- bonus in your request?
Factual experience
Helpful hint

27. Ensuring a return on loyalty 179
Myths about customer loyalty programmes
Establishing your own corporate loyalty programme
Factual experience
Helpful hint

28. Protect your intellectual property or watch it 185
vanish overnight
Types of intellectual properties
Legal forms of protection
When protection is unavailable
Factual experience
Helpful hint

29. Being in the right place at the right time 191
Searching for opportunities within your orbit of experience
Carving a niche by matching opportunity to expertise
Factual experience
Helpful hint

30. Strategies for efficient cash flow management............... 197
    Solving cash flow problems
    Factual experience
    Helpful hint

31. Monitoring growth using an audit checklist 203
    How to use the audit for maximum effectiveness
    The audit analysis
    The management audit
    The operations audit
    The financial audit

Epilogue 223
Glossary of business terms 227
Business address book ....
More useful reading ....
Index ....

Preface

There are ten deadly mistakes you can make in minding your own business

If not detected and rectified, they spread like a cancer. This book starts off by identifying these insidious traps and how you can avoid their intrusion into your affairs.

It goes further though, much further, by providing you with a stream of tried and tested strategies to ensure steady progress for your enterprise irrespective of changes in market forces. The universal failure rate in business is now reaching staggering proportions (most especially among start-ups) but those entrepreneurs who consciously or unwittingly employ these age-old strategies remain proactive in all kinds of weather because they always recognise the storm signals and react accordingly.

As you will observe as you read these pages, I never stayed for too long in one place. I have a tendency to react to new ideas and new challenges, but always within my own area of expertise.

Jim Green

Prologue

How to avoid the ten most deadly mistakes in minding your own business

Why are we opening a book on the subject of strategy with a review of deadly mistakes?

Because the 30 power-laden strategies you will learn as you course through these pages are devised from ten quantifiable mistakes that have pulled down many a promising enterprise. Whether you have been in business for years or are just starting out, you need to recognise these costly errors before you can avoid them.

These then are the deadly traps that too many small business owners fall into:

1. Getting wedded to an idea and sticking with it for too long - Don't stay married for life to a single idea. Ideas are the currency of entrepreneurs. Play around with as many ideas as you like to discover which ones create money and lasting success.
2. Operating without a viable marketing plan - A winning marketing plan captures the attention you need to surround your enterprise with the right calibre of people; employees, customers, suppliers. There may be a 100 disparate ways to market your business but an exclusive viable plan implemented effectively,

efficiently, and consistently will be results driven, eliminating guesswork.
3. Failing to appreciate market forces - Changes in customer preferences and advances in competitive products and services can leave you stranded in the dust unless you take the trouble to get to know your market and your customers well. It is essential that you appreciate what customers want now, what they're likely to want in the future, how their buying patterns are evolving, and how you can become a constant resource for them even if you don't have the right products and services for them right now.
4. Ignoring your cash position - Customers do not always respond to superior products in the time frame that you think they should. You'll need plenty of cash to sustain operations in the interim. Cash is king, so be on your guard as to how it flows in - and out.
5. Ignoring employees - The management and motivation of staff is one of the biggest challenges facing the business owner. Without patience, persistence and people skills, problems quickly multiply - and morale, productivity and profits can easily be destroyed. Always make your people your first priority.
6. Confusing likelihood with reality - The successful entrepreneur lives in the world of likelihood but spends money in the real world. Be realistic in all of your commercial undertakings.
7. Operating without a sales strategy - Without a strategy for selling, there is no effective way to gauge the financial growth and progress of a business. You need a realistic map that identifies where the sales

will come from, how they will come - and from whom.
8. Playing the Lone Ranger with no back up - You are the key to it all but you cannot do everything yourself and continue to grow at the same time. Even modest success can overwhelm you unless you hire the right staff and delegate responsibility.
9. Operating with no mastermind on board - Most small businesses expand faster when there is someone around with a few grey hairs to cast an experienced eye occasionally on overall activity. Your elder statesperson could operate for you as an executive director or part-time consultant.
10. Giving up - Not every successful entrepreneur gets it right first time; some fail several times before they strike the core formula that does it for them. So, if you are failing, go ahead and fail. But fail fast and learn from the experience. Then try again with this new wisdom. Never give up and never suffer either.

KNOWLEDGE IS THE KEY

The birds of the air have the knowledge (and the wings) to get from one destination to another on time, every time. They have no need of travel schedules, passports, currency exchange, traveller cheques, or any other restrictive man-made paraphernalia to staunch their progress. Flocks of swifts, for example, are so confident of their navigational prowess they catnap on the wing on journeys spanning thousands of miles.

They have an instinctive fail-safe route plan.
So too will you when you have absorbed the strategies set out in this book because you will have the knowledge and the wings to avoid the ten most deadly mistakes in minding your own business. The first 10 chapters address these deadly traps head on and the 20 chapters that follow will provide you with a stream of proven strategies to ensure your ongoing success.

PART 1
TACKLING THE DEADLY MISTAKES HEAD ON

Chapter 1

Broadening your horizons generates new ideas

In a speech he made on March 14 2002, The Chancellor of the Exchequer Gordon Brown MP made this statement in his chastisement of the Big Banks failure to properly service the basic financial requirements of small business.

> *"There are over 3.5million UK small businesses representing 55 per cent of jobs, 50 per cent of all business turnover, and economic activity of £1trillion a year"*

If you were ever in need of affirmation on the validity of your vocation, now you have the measure of your importance as a small business operator in the eyes of Her Majesty's Government. This is heartening news *but* 3.5million small businesses did not just happen as a natural course of events; their beginnings, their viability, their future, all depend to a large extent on an ever perpetuating well of workable new ideas.

Now read this extract from an article which appeared around the same time in the medical journal *The Lancet:*

> *"On reaching the age of seventy five, the average person retains 97 per cent of the brain cells that were in evidence at the age of twenty five"*

Considered separately, these statements are unconnected; combined they present a powerful concept.

- Ideas are what make small business big in terms of job creation, turnover and overall market share
- You have the propensity to keep on generating new ideas until well beyond retirement age

Now there is a concept to treasure as a small business owner.

BROADENING HORIZONS WITHIN YOUR OWN AREA OF EXPERTISE

Broadening your horizons does not advocate launching out into commercial areas where you possess neither the required knowledge nor the experience to survive let alone succeed. Such venturing is folly, save for a select band of high risk taking entrepreneurial nomads. Your own backyard, your particular area of expertise is where you should be concentrating your efforts on generating a consistent flow of ideas, ideas essential to your future prosperity. There are sufficient openings in whatever you do right now to carve out new opportunities, to develop new profit centres.

> *"I run a corner shop. What new ideas could I generate for my static business?"*

You could think of various possibilities for improvement…

- **Re-appraise your stock strategy** - Cut out the deadwood, focus on the staples; introduce additional, proven fast moving lines.
- **Reorganise your displays** - Make self-service a pleasure as opposed to an obstacle course for your customers.

- **Improve store lighting** - Facilitate for easier browsing and double your chances of grabbing impulse buyers.
- **Give the place a makeover** - Just a lick of paint here and there could turn your outlet into a home from home.
- **Plan to increase your footfall** - Apply for a Paypoint or Payzone facility and, if successful, you are guaranteed a significant increase in daily store traffic; people dropping in to pay utility accounts and making impulse purchases along the way. You'll also receive a small commission payment on each transaction = additional profit centre.
- **Build a (e) mailing list** - Get to know your regulars well enough to get their email addresses (most of them have at least one). Email them weekly with special offers, discounted deals, etc.
- **Set up a web site** - So you'll be on the World Wide Web, so what? Advertise your site instore and just watch what happens next. Use a free service and you can build as many pages as you like for free - and host them for free.
- **Start a 'menage' or family club** - They still work and they pull in up cash front.

You could think up all sorts of other useful ideas - if you apply yourself...

TAPPING INTO YOUR INNATE FOUNTAIN OF NEW IDEAS

Regardless of the nature of your own small business initiative, it contains a fountain of new commercial possibilities just waiting to be tapped. And you can tap into them if you try because you are a compendium of innate skills and inventiveness. Start working now on generating some new ideas - but do not be discouraged if they don't work right off. It took Edison over 1000 ideas before he invented the light bulb and John Logie Baird toiled away for over a decade before he brought the world the wonder of television.

Yours is a more modest remit. Look closely at your business to determine how, where and when you could broaden your horizons. Just one good idea, once in a while, could make all the difference.

WHEN YOU COME UP WITH AN IDEA

As with most things in life, you have a choice.
- If it's feasible - go for it
- If it's not - discard it

Or

- Don't discard the no-no but keep it the back burner for future reference…

FACTUAL EXPERIENCE

I was only interested in two subjects at school: **Art** and appreciation of the **English** language - and I've been making my living from them ever since. As a result, I've spent most of my life in the right hand side of my brain, switching occasionally to the left brain to handle practicalities. In the process I've had many careers, but I have never discarded any of the acquired knowledge. The skills applicable in one walk of life have a habit of replicating themselves in the context of other opportunities that happen along.

I've founded, managed, bought and sold many businesses over the years - but for your information, here is what I'm up to currently...

- **Marketing services** - catering for a small but disparate clientele (voluntary basis)
- **Developing trading names** and rationales for effective application
- **Internet** - creating, designing, building commercial web sites
- **Writing** - published titles in both fiction and non-fiction genres
- **Magazines** -contributions to consumer interest periodicals
- **Lecturing** - on a variety of business oriented platforms
- **Book reviews** - reviewing other people's work in quality journals
- **Book titles** - devising titles for other people's produce
- **Book covers** - designing jackets to a prescribed brief
- **Watercolourist** - in my spare time...

You will note something in common with all of these activities. They have to do with creativity, which is in effect the only thing I really know *anything* about.

It was the creative urge that impelled me once to broaden my horizons and do something I'd always wanted to do: produce a motion picture. *Towards The Morning* (Filmessence 1980) starred Hywel Bennett, Judy Geeson and Michael Kitchen. This forty-minute programmer supported the feature film *Eye Of The Needle* in cinemas throughout the world.

I not only realised my ambition but I also recouped my investment with a little to spare. Why am I telling you this? Certainly not to impress, but to illustrate how keeping the brain active on a variety of fronts has the knock-on effect of kick starting the generation of new ideas.

Never neglect your own propensity to broaden the prevailing horizons and generate new ideas to add colour to future happenings.

HELPFUL HINT

Always have pad and pen to hand wherever you are, day and night. Ideas flash into the mind at the most unexpected times and to make the most of them, you must write down the gist as it filters through. This is how to use your innate well of inspiration to best advantage. It always welcomes you with open arms and your job is to polish the raw material provided into practical, workable concepts.

Chapter 2

Nurturing the plan that never stops evolving

Sound though some of them may be, your stream of new ideas won't get you very far unless orchestrated by a viable plan for realisation, a plan that never stops evolving.

Before we delve into the planning process though, let's have a quick stab at a basic definition. **Marketing is absolutely everything connected with the corporate process that determines whether a potential customer makes a conscious decision to buy, or not to buy, as the case may be.**

Walk into your local Waterstones, Borders or WHS, scan the myriad of titles on the overloaded shelves in the marketing section, and you might reasonably wonder if it could be as simple as that. But it is. Much gunge is produced on the subject of marketing and much of it is based on little more than highfalutin jargon designed to keep the pundits in business than to help small business in the real world.

Your marketing plan will not come out of any book.

YOUR PLAN STARTS AND ENDS WITH YOU

It will start and end with you because only you know how to construct and develop it.

The plan you will devise will be perpetual, not some piece of glitz to be flashed around for additional funding, then stuffed away in a drawer and forgotten. At the outset it can be as modest as two or three sheets of foolscap because it will grow and evolve in time as you lay down new and essential parameters to guide you on the rocky road that lies ahead. It will of course contain the usual nuts and bolts but it will also include something of much more intrinsic value. This master plan will highlight your own personal philosophy on how the business will realistically progress in tandem with your aspirations.

You will live, eat and sleep with your master marketing plan for all of your working life. It will become your personal bible but unlike *The Bible*, it will not be written in tablets of stone; it will be forever changing, forever evolving, forever improving, forever updating as exciting new ideas and developments come on stream

WHERE TO BEGIN

Right where you are right now, with yourself; you are the lynchpin upon which all the other elements have their being. Shining through the plan will be your personality, your aspirations and your strategies for the present security and future growth of the enterprise. You are not setting out to flash your plan around to all and sundry but through its consistent **enactment** people will come to know you for what you represent: a professional small business operator who appreciates where the business is at and where it is heading. In the process you will attract the right calibre of people around you: customers, suppliers, employees. This is all part of the **corporate process** highlighted in our definition of marketing.

When you are selling, you are marketing, and what you are marketing is not products or services, it's **you**, and you will be selling *you* in everything you undertake in your marketing activities for the rest of your working life.

How you project to others, how you dress, how you speak, how you earn (not command) respect, these are the essential facets of basic marketing.

You are unique because you are you. Always make the most of you.

SLOTTING IN THE NUTS AND BOLTS

Now let's move on to what many misguided optimists believe constitutes commercial marketing: the nuts and bolts. These are important practical elements but they are not the be-and-end-all. They just require slotting in as and when required.

From the list below, you will certainly want to include the first three and some of the others in your plan, and to be reviewing and revising their usefulness on a regular basis. Whichever currently apply in your particular enterprise, do not be tempted to stick rigidly to them. What worked last year won't necessarily cut the mustard this year; play safe and evaluate every new option that comes your way.

- **Buying policy**
- **Selling policy**
- **Distribution policy**
- **Advertising**
- **Promotions**
- **Premiums**
- **Exhibitions**
- **Public relations**

Marketing is a common sense approach to conducting your business. It starts and ends with you: how you project, how you deal with customers, how you handle suppliers, how you treat your staff. In short, what sort of image you create for yourself and your enterprise.

FACTUAL EXPERIENCE

My first marketing services venture came into the world as a premature birth.

It happened this way: Late one Friday afternoon I was summonsed before the managing director of the advertising agency that employed me. He had heard on the grapevine that I was *thinking* about setting up on my own, and so he decided to give me a lift by booting me out on the street, there and then.

I had no business plan, no marketing plan, and no premises. What I did have though was a little funding and a guaranteed clientele (including some of his). Progress in my fledgling enterprise was erratic in the early months but despite my lack of preparation (or perhaps because of it) the business soon began to flourish, as did my propensity for planning ahead for the future. In retrospect, my late employer had done me a favour. He had taught me how to swim by chucking me in head first at the deep end, and although I survived the initial impact and mastered sufficient basic strokes to find my way around the big fish in the pond, I could just as easily disappeared without a trace down the plug hole.

The lesson I learned (and it has stayed with me ever since) is that when you have a cunning plan, or opportunity comes calling, or the brilliant idea suddenly flashes into your mind, get it all down in writing fast in the shape of a plan, a marketing plan. Then keep on adding to it, and adding to it, forevermore

HELPFUL HINT

Don't fall into the deadly trap that many others do; abandoning your business plan almost as soon as the enterprise is underway. Treat it as sacrosanct and use it every day to guide you safely through the twists and turns of commercial progression.

Chapter 3

Moving with the times stops you lagging behind

The day you stop learning in business is the day you should start making plans for a closing down sale. Nothing stands still; nothing ever did.

Lightning fast advances in technology blow away in their wake long established business practices. Who for instance would want to go cap in hand tomorrow looking for funding to invest in a carbon paper manufacturing plant? Or set up as a jobbing printer or process engraver of printing blocks? There is still a market of sorts for all three but it has shrunk alarmingly in tandem with the growth of computer technology. The global demand for iron, steel and coal has also diminished significantly and these utilities no longer have the market penetration they enjoyed for centuries.

Market forces rule and those who ignore them do so at their peril.

But fads and fashions can also exert equally punitive consequences.

Back in 1934 when Columbia Pictures released *It Happened One Night* on an unsuspecting movie-going public, no one had an inkling of the damage one simple ten second scene would inflict on the garment industry. When Clark Gable peeled off his shirt to display a bare chest, sales of men's vests nose dived all over the world. Wives, girlfriends and partners were the architects of this alarming slump and it took the industry several years of heavy counter promotion before they made up for lost ground.

Could market forces, fads and fashions have an impact in the industry or service in which you operate? They could, and they frequently do, even in the smallest of commercial sectors.

KEEPING AN OPEN EYE ON YOUR COMPETITION

As good a barometer as any on keeping tabs on what's happening all around you is to monitor competitive activity. It's easy to develop tunnel vision when focusing on your own little corner of the market; focusing so hard that you fail to pick up telltale signals such as subtle changes in consumer preferences and advances in competitive products and services. Such undetected happenings can leave you struggling to catch up.

Instigate your own press cuttings service - Don't just scan through the trade journals; start reading them from cover to cover. Cut out articles of current and future interest; paste them into a ledger for future reference. Repeat the exercise for relevant local press. Do not pass this chore over to an employee or a cuttings agency. Only you know what to look for and only you can make use of the accumulated intelligence.

Ask around your clientele - They won't mind. In fact, they will open up. If they're getting good service, they will tell you, and you should take careful note because otherwise they may be handing out your share to someone else tomorrow. If they are not enjoying good service, they will also tell you - and there is your opportunity.

Take especial note when they talk about *their* customers. Look out for indicators on changes in consumer preferences because they have a direct influence on your current and future production plans.

KEEPING PACE WITH THE CYBERSPACE OPPORTUNITY

Despite the bad publicity associated with the collapse of numerous dot.coms in recent times, the Internet is still in its infancy and yet still offers an incredible opportunity to small business - if small business would take the trouble to discover how best to use the cyberspace medium to its *current* advantage. In so doing, small businesses will be operating on a universal platform and on equal status to the major players. That said, unless yours is a downloadable product or service, you won't be doing much in the way of direct selling (not yet anyway) but you will move with the times and carve out a niche for yourself in other essential directions.

MAKING THE INTERNET WORK FOR YOU

How do you do that? How do you make the Net work for you in your business operation? And **what's in it for you?**

Here's how someone viewed the situation a few years back…

> *"If you're not doing business on the Internet by the year 2000,*
>
> you won't be doing business"
> Bill Gates

Bill Gates' prediction failed to materialise. Perhaps he allowed personal vanity to overrule his sanity because there are hundreds of thousands of commercial concerns worldwide who don't do **any** business on the Internet and yet continue to prosper.

But that does not mean to say that these businesses don't make best use of the Net. **Most of them do.**

So, how do you make the Net work for you?

Use it for the purpose for which it was invented. Use it as a channel of information.

- A channel for **receivable** information
- A channel for **deliverable** information.

Doing it this way provides you with two valuable operational devices

The facility to receive information opens the door to ongoing **market research** while the facility to deliver information electronically presents you with a **cyberspace marketing application.**

Using the Internet search facilities, you can keep tabs on the marketplace, trends, and what the competition is up to. You can source valuable applications and software – and all for free. You can be on constant lookout for trading opportunities.

Using the Net as a marketing application, you can create a powerful web site.

- To promote your merchandise
- To foster customer loyalty
- To service their requirements

- To capture email addresses that build up into lists of potential customers.

You can do all of this - and if you go about matters in the right way, **you can do it all for free.**

THE VALUE OF A GOOD WEB SITE

These are the benefits you should be looking to accrue from your web site, a fusion of incoming and outgoing information, intelligence that you should embrace to service existing customers and attract new ones. And unlike printed matter, you need never be nervous about imparting sensitive information (price lists, specifications, etc) because you have the facility to update variable data instantly.

As for direct selling, you'll get an odd sale or two from your site, but not a lot. Not yet anyway. Stick with it though, and **you'll do much more direct selling in time**, as the retail ethos of the web begins to bite.

And here is how it all pans out in the creation of the site
- Your mission statement and complementary graphics on the home page - where you would also position an **'order' button**
- Appropriate content for the pages devoted to produce, sales and service
- Something of value for your web site visitors – useful tips which should be updated on a regular basis
- Links from one page to another within your site - **but not beyond** - or you'll lose your precious visitors
- A guest book where visitors can clock in and record comments

- A dedicated search engine to help them find their way around your site
- An email address where they can contact you – and finally
- A facility to which you should give serious consideration, an invitation to subscribe to your **free ezine**

Okay, there's some work involved in servicing the final item listed – but it will be worth it – because ezines (electronic newsletters) are the best way to capture email addresses, build up a prospects list, and create potential customers.

As to costs for web site creation and hosting; zero, if you use www.freeservers.com

Here is what you get with the basic plan

- 20 megabytes – enough to house all of your pages with some to spare
- Free hosting, domain name, web based email
- The easiest page-building tools I have ever encountered
- Guest books, counters, form e-mailers, tutorials

Spend a few pounds a month with them and they'll give you even more advanced tools to create a web site which looks as though it cost £25,000 to construct.

FACTUAL EXPERIENCE

A brush with advancing technology all of 30 years ago saved me losing my biggest customer. Loyds Retailers was based in Manchester and my little agency was 235 miles away. I had won the business against all the odds and had been successfully servicing it for four years, flying down every Monday and Friday morning for instructions and enacting them when I got back home in the early evening.

Then the client appointed a new marketing director and I began to hear rumblings about expensive telephone calls and inaccessibility because of the distance factor.

As I pondered the threat to my tenure on the account, a young lady representative (rare in those days) walked into the agency requesting permission to demonstrate a newfangled device for transmitting text and images to destinations hundreds of miles away. This prototype of the modern fax (then known as the telecopier) was the answer to an adman's prayer and I ordered machines to be installed in both the client's and our own premises. They were cumbersome 'hand-cranked' devices but they added a sense of immediacy to communications. What the new marketing director really wanted was for me to open an office in Manchester but he relented now that he was receiving reports, press ad layouts and text *before* we got together for our face-to-face meetings.

This act of moving with the times doesn't seem like much these days but it meant a lot then in a time when mobiles, emailing, the Internet, inter alia, were yet to be invented.

HELPFUL HINT

Getting up to speed with the advances in technology isn't enough; you must also keep pace. Changes occur at the speed of light and what worked as a marketing application yesterday will not necessarily cut the mustard for you tomorrow. Keep learning, keep experimenting, and above all master the facility for using the Internet to serve your customers the better, to inform them, to educate them.

Chapter 4

Control the cash or risk certain closure

To ensure safe passage in the often-turbulent seas of commercial venturing, you must become confident in your own ability to control cash. For most entrepreneurs this is not a problem but for those of us of a right brain disposition, it can be problematic. Simple or difficult, the concept has to be grasped. It will matter not a jot how brilliant your marketing strategy is if you fail to control the cash because all you will be achieving is a few steps closer to oblivion.

WHY CASH IS KING

What you take in, what you pay out - that's cash flow management.

But some small business owners tend to confuse cash flow with profit. Cash and profit are not the same thing. Profit always includes a number of **non-cash items** like depreciation and accruals (costs you have included but not yet paid out because you are still awaiting invoices).

Cash flow is a simpler concept. It is the balance between cash you have received (from customers and other sources) less cash you have paid out (to suppliers and employees).

Established businesses that go bust do so because they have run out of cash, not because they are unprofitable. On paper they may be showing a handsome profit but they drop out of the race because they fail to manage their cash flow.

WHY YOU MUST KEEP A CASH BOOK

You don't require to be an accountant to calculate your cash flow quickly and at any given point. In fact, it is crucial that you know exactly how much cash is in the business every day. Simply keep a cash book into which you religiously record all daily transactions: cash received (cash/cheques/whatever) and the cash you have paid out.

STRUCTURING YOUR CASH FLOW TO BEST EFFECT

Getting the cash flow right is critical and keeping it on the right track is even more crucial. But how can you achieve that when you are not self-financing? There is a way, a very sensible way.

> *Endeavour to structure your cash flow in such a way that the bulk of the cash comes in before you have to pay out. That way you will be working on other people's money, interest free.*

Can't be done? Yes it can. I've managed it in every business I've ever been associated with.

PAYING YOUR WAY

Take as much credit as your suppliers will allow but in return for their forbearance always pay them on the agreed date. Do it this way and when the time comes around when you need a little more time to cough up, you are more likely to have your request granted. Trust and integrity, they go hand in glove.

COLLECTING DUES

Cash coming in less regularly than you are shelling out spells trouble…

Never be afraid to ask for what you are due, when it is due. Be explicit though as to *exactly* what your payment terms are and keep on reminding your creditors on every invoice and every statement you send out. All the good service you are providing won't amount to a row of runner beans if you neglect to get the cash in on time, every time. It has to do with conditioning. You'll get your invoices nearer to the top of the pile each month if you condition your customers and keep on conditioning them. In time they will come to respect your persistence (grudgingly perhaps) but they will become conditioned to paying you on the due date.

For the odd customer who pays no heed, fire off a judgement summons without prior warning. That has a sobering effect on persistent defaulters and invariably results in you collecting your dues with incurring court costs.

WHY TILL DIPPING IS A NO-NO

You may not operate your business affairs with a tangible cash register but you have at your command a hypothetical till which you may be tempted to raid now and again. Don't do it. It's a mug's game and the only person you'll be thieving from is yourself. Till dipping has its comeuppance because sooner or later you will called to account for your light fingering and the people you will be accounting to will be your creditors.

NEVER TRY TO TRADE YOUR WAY OUT OF TROUBLE

Trading your way out of trouble means taking on bigger amounts of new business in order to pay off old debts; it's the road to ruin because your total outstanding commitments will inevitably increase and multiply. Avoid the temptation to trade your way out of trouble. Concentrate rather on resolving the underlying reasons why the business is underachieving.

FACTUAL EXPERIENCE

I once founded, managed, and eventually sold on a business that by the very nature of its trading strategy was the perfect panacea for ensuring efficient cash flow management. The concept was specialised publishing - the market was local government councils - and the revenue source was advertising contracts from local businesses.

Here is how it worked.

I was in the business of supplying local authorities with information handbooks (guides, maps, planning, environmental, etc) for local consumption. The authorities paid out no cash for the published produce and in return granted me exclusive advertising rights. Now here is where it gets interesting in the context of cash flow control.

All advertising contracts negotiated were on the strict basis (unlike conventional publishing contracts) of payment within **seven days** of receipt of signed documentation. Conversely, payment to suppliers (origination and printing) was not due until delivery of produce. My only other outgoing on these exercises was weekly commission payments to teams of self-employed sales agents which amounted to less than 20 per cent of the total weekly incoming.

Have a close look at your strategy for collecting dues and paying suppliers - then determine whether you could get the cash in quicker than you are currently shelling it out.

HELPFUL HINT

Come to terms with the money thing early in your career as a self-starting operator and it will serve you well in the long run. There is no mystique about controlling cash flow nor is absolute control difficult to achieve. It is a matter of discipline and practical application, adherence to which will ensure safe passage for your enterprise. Neglect, on the other hand, guarantees certain failure.

Chapter 5

Keeping good employees and promoting from within

Some businesses appear to operate a revolving door policy in the matter of staff recruitment (in one end and out the other) while others have people lining up to join.

Are there secrets to procuring and keeping the best people? Not really; it's a common sense approach. The management and motivation of staff is one of the biggest challenges facing the small business owner. Without patience, persistence and people skills, problems quickly multiply - and morale, productivity and profits can easily be destroyed.

Always make your people your first priority, treat them with respect, train them, and reward them regularly for good service provided.

GETTING GOOD STAFF IN THE FIRST PLACE

Although interviewing can be a laborious process, doing it well is worth the time and effort because every time you bring a new person into the mix of your staff, it changes the dynamic and you want to be sure it changes for the better.

Another (sometimes more productive) way to find good staff is to ask around your current employees as to who they would like to work with. Some businesses even offer incentives to trusted members of staff who introduce employees that stay with the company for a minimum amount of time, say three months. New starts introduced by fellow employees have the advantage of some prior knowledge about what to expect in your operation. In addition, they already have a friend on staff, so they are more likely to feel at home more quickly.

CREATIVE WAYS TO REWARD YOUR EMPLOYEES

Sometimes you just aren't ready to grow as fast as you would like nor do you have the resources to offer 'stellar' employees regular pay increases. But you can reward their good service in other little ways, creative ways, within the confines of your budget; a flash bonus, theatre/film tickets for the family, stand seats at sporting events, etc. Good employees are not out to screw you at every turn; they just like to be shown some appreciation now and again.

> *Look after your staff and they will look after your business.*

IMPARTING YOUR OWN WISDOM TO HELP THEM GROW

Never hold back from teaching your staff the tricks of the trade. Some employers do hold back out of a sense of insecurity but this is bad business practice. Impart in employees your own philosophy of the enterprise, tell them your aspirations and demonstrate how they can help you achieve them. Be totally honest, warts and all, and you will be helping them to grow and mature in your shadow.

WHEN GOOD EMPLOYEES OUTGROW THEIR POSITIONS

When you hire good people, you leave yourself open to the risk that their abilities will in time outpace the job specification. You have three choices...

- Let them go
- Promote them
- Expand your business to make room for their expertise

The last option might sound risky especially if you are not yet ready to expand - but **wouldn't you rather put the skills of an experienced, talented employee to best use in helping you grow rather than risk losing a rising star?**

CUTTING LOOSE THE DEADWOOD

You have to be pragmatic about this.

- If someone is consistently under-performing and costing you money into the bargain, cut your losses and get rid of him/her without delay.
- If someone is consistently causing trouble, adversely affecting morale and the work ethic, get shot of the offender.

However, when it is a case of an employee who simply needs more training, then go out of your way to provide whatever is required. Consider pairing the individual with an exemplary employee to assist with the training.

HELPING EMPLOYEES TO MOVE ON

Always be aware that (if you are doing your own job properly) certain wide-awake members of staff will develop the confidence to move on to the next dream job when they have outgrown your employment. Assist them to realise their ambitions. Good ex-employees are the best source of referrals and their going makes room for the next rising stars in your team to move up a peg.

Some too will depart to replicate on their own account what you are doing. Treat their leaving with good grace because they are living monuments to your ability to train others to grow in stature.

PROMOTING FROM WITHIN

Promoting from within (or 'rolling your own') is always the best option when you are on an expansion kick. You don't have to worry about capability or the validity of the curriculum vitae. You had a hand in developing both. Here are a few wrinkles to assist you in spotting likely prospects for promotion from within.

- **Test out staff** by gradually adding more responsibilities. If an employee can handle new tasks, he/she may be ready to move up the ladder.
- **Speak to your employees to ascertain their goals**, their career aspirations, and their ideas for the company. This information can help determine if higher-level positions are something they would be comfortable with and desire.

- **Observe and work with employees** to discover any special skills that would make them attractive candidates for another position in the company.
- **Develop a plan to replace promoted workers.** Some companies use internships to attract employees; for example, taking on students during scholastic breaks.
- In-house training programmes are also beneficial.

Promoting from within is a viable, money-saving option. Learn to recognise the talent that is right there in front of you and take advantage of it. The end result: happier employees and lower recruitment costs.

FACTUAL EXPERIENCE

Over the years I have engaged staff in numbers ranging from one to forty. I've had people work for me who would walk through walls of fire without thought of reward; I've had others who would do it if the price was right; I've had one or two who would have ruined (or stolen) my business if I had allowed them.

I've loved them all (save those few) and I always rolled my own, rarely sourcing externally unless it happened to be for a recognised star.

Regrettably, I've lost touch with most of them but I watch with satisfaction the progress of a few who have gone on to do greater and better things than I ever managed to achieve.

When you start out and there's only a handful in the gang, it's much easier to develop and retain the family ethos. As you grow, surround yourself with good managers to do what you no longer can to the utmost effect: keeping an eye on everyone else…

HELPFUL HINT

When I started out in my first enterprise at the age of fifteen, an elder statesman enquired of me as to what I reckoned was the single most important aspect of conducting business. 'Profit,' I replied brashly. 'No,' he said. 'People.' He was right and all I got right was the initial letter of the vital aspect. Without good people around you, the profit motive doesn't come into the equation; it's too busy struggling to leave the starting gate.

Chapter 6
Living out each day of your retirement to its fullest measure

You'll come across several references in this book to the left and right hand sides of the brain. No one is totally left-brained or totally right-brained **but** just as you have a dominant hand, dominant eye, dominant foot, you also have a dominant side of the brain (although not necessarily the one you prefer). Acknowledged geniuses would appear to be able to spend almost all of their life in one or other side, producing the most astonishing achievements in the realms of art, music, literature, science, architecture, etc. For mere mortals though, a compatible fusion between both sides of the brain is an essential requirement for living comfortably in the real world of hard tack commerce.

OPERATING ON THE LEFT HAND SIDE OF THE BRAIN

This is where the hard graft occurs and it's where most business people operate as they go about workaday tasks. It's where you do your reasoning, working out and adding up, and it's where you choose every word you utter.

Characteristics of the left brain
- It reasons step-by-step
- It is logical
- It is mathematical

- It is talkative
- It uses patterns
- It dominates the right brain

Note the final characteristic and you will appreciate why most people operate in the left brain most of the time.

OPERATING ON THE RIGHT HAND CHANNEL

You switch to the right hand channel when you enter the wild blue yonder: creating ideas and visualising new developments. For some the switch is easy, for others not so easy.

Characteristics of the right brain

- It is mystical
- It is musical
- It is creative
- It is pictorial
- It seeks patterns
- It is submissive to the left brain

If the left brain doesn't feel like switching over, it won't budge.

CONFUSING LIKELIHOOD WITH REALITY

Because of these conflicting characteristics between left and right, problems can arise, causing us to confuse likelihood with reality.

- **Spend all the time in your left brain and you could miss out on opportunity**
- **Spend all the time in your right brain and you could blow your business**

The catch is that in order to get the most from your brain, you need to use both sides efficiently and effectively.

You can and must develop both sides of the brain.

STRIKING A BALANCE BETWEEN THE THOUGHT PROCESSES

Mind power is awesome when you learn to strike a balance between the thought processes. We all live in a mind world and how each of us sees in the mind's eye what's happening out there in the real world actually makes it how it is. We look at the world through our own eyes and immediately start making judgements solely on the evidence of what we *think* we see. In other words, we interpret situations as they occur in our lives. If we're not careful, mind power can work against us if we fall into the habit of permanently locking ourselves into one side of the brain.

To use mind power effectively, strike an equitable balance between the left and right hand sides of the brain.

BECOMING CENTERED AND SINGLE-MINDED IN DECISION MAKING

Conversely, when facing vexatious decisions, try to bypass both states of consciousness (left and right hand sides of the brain) and dig deeply but calmly into your subconscious.

To maintain a connection with this wellspring of wisdom, you must be able to concentrate. Given the roving, restless nature of the conscious mind, it takes will and skill to achieve true focus. If you've grown up on a steady diet of television, remote control in hand, you're probably used to seeing life in two-second sound bites, and your attention span is miniscule. Intuition cannot flow in a noisy, chaotic world, so first try reducing the amount of stimuli you take in each day. Then narrow it all down gradually and you will discover that you are able to concentrate calmly on the task in hand. Start by focusing your attention fully *inside* your body—this will help you access your own deepest knowledge.

You will be able to determine for yourself the power that centring can exert on your everyday affairs when you read Chapter 25 on the subject of Intuition.

FACTUAL EXPERIENCE

As you may have already guessed, my own preferred state of mind rests in the right brain and I have always had to work hard at maintaining that elusive but essential equitable balance between the thought processes. Mathematics, for example, remains a mystery to me, and I can lay no claim to academic qualifications in simple arithmetic, algebra or geometry. What I have accomplished though is mastery over the balance sheet but I only manage that through switching to the right brain…

Accordingly, I have always surrounded myself in business with a modicum of left-brain oriented colleagues who provide a service that I cannot.

It is hard work but there is no other way; you must learn how to use both sides of the brain within your own limitations in order to avoid mixing up likelihood with reality.

HELPFUL HINT

While it is more comfortable to reside in that side of the brain that appears to provide the most stimulus; it is nevertheless essential to master living in both sides if you are to be constantly in control of your destiny. Practice the art of striking a balance between the thought processes and strive to become single-minded in decision making.

Chapter 7

There's no sale until the cash is in the bank

Most start-ups that go under do so because they pay scant attention to the very business plan they worked so painstakingly to develop; most established businesses that go under do so because they have no predefined sales plan. Without a strategy for selling, there is no effective way to gauge the financial growth and progress of a business.

You need a realistic map that identifies:

- **Where the sales will come from**
- **How they will arrive**
- **Who will provide the sales**

But never lose sight of the fact that even when you have established these requirements to your satisfaction, the 'no sale' sign will still be showing until the cash is in the bank.

DETERMINING YOUR PRICING STRATEGY

It is your privilege to create the policies that set your selling prices but bear in mind that your pricing strategy is dependent upon a variety of factors. Think it all out before you set your SPs (selling prices) in concrete.

FORECASTING AND TARGETING SALES

You must forecast and target your sales - by season, by calendar event, even by time of day. You need to know how your venture will generate sales over a given period of time. The sales forecast (budgeted sales) will be important data for your cash flow projection. It appears at the top and is the catalyst to what appears in your bottom line. These targets will help to determine priorities and channel your energies accordingly.

Perhaps you haven't had a stab so far at forecasting and targeting sales in an orderly fashion, so how can you estimate? Here is how you do it.

- **Observe your competitors** - Try to gather intelligence on the typical spend per customer.
- **What are your estimates for customers per month**? - Work out your market share. First, estimate the number of customers who buy from businesses like yours within the immediate catchment area. Now work out how many times each of these customers buys in a year (9 small ads, 3 hours of plumbing, etc). Now multiply the two numbers to establish the total size of the market. Finally, divide your sales into the total market size to get your market share.
- **What is your capacity?** - Maximum production output of your knobblewockers, number of rooms in the hotel, number of tuition slots in the appointments book? What percentage utilisation do you expect to achieve in each month of each sales period? Work this out by market segment. Estimate the average spend per customer.
- **List all firm orders** you have generated.

Sales build up from small beginnings **but** they may be affected by fluctuations in the national economy: levels of unemployment, rising interest rates etc. For example, If you are selling to account customers, your profit and loss forecast must reveal all the sales you have **invoiced out but for which no payment has yet been received**. Some customers may turn out to be bad debts.

APPRECIATING THE NATURE OF YOUR SALES MACHINE

Your operational plan should reveal your sales machine.
- Who will do the selling?
- How are sales and promotions linked?
- What expertise is required?
- Does selling involve lots of design work and submission of quotations? If so, generation of these is a necessary cost before any sales are secured.
- For the sole proprietor (for example, a kitchen or double-glazing installer) such design and selling work may be outside of production hours. When a client has to be visited or spoken to in the workshop no other work can be done. Allow for that.
- What systems will be required to support the sales effort e.g. a point-of-sale system?

WHY THERE IS NO SALE UNTIL YOU COLLECT YOUR DUES

In Chapter 4 we discussed the importance of cash control in your everyday activities.

If the bulk of your business is transacted on account, go back and re-read the section on collecting dues. All your sales forecasting and targeting will go for naught if you don't get the cash in on the due date of every month. Alternatively, if your customers settle up at the point of sale, record these incomings in your cash book every day.

FACTUAL EXPERIENCE

Accurate forecasting is so vital that I operate my businesses on weekly (sometimes daily) profit and loss statements. That way I can easily and quickly spot irregularities such as fluctuations I had not/could not previously account for. As the bulk of the operating expenses are fixed, it is invariably in the top line that these fluctuations occur.

Devising the sales strategy isn't something you attend to at the beginning of the period; you should be dissecting, honing and polishing the plan every day.

HELPFUL HINT

No one will ever be in danger of getting knocked over in the rush for your produce unless you have a clinical campaign of action for its profitable disposal. Your plan must pinpoint the precise market segments and how, when, and why customers will buy from you. Never leave the sales function to chance; plan to make it happen and ensure that your plan legislates for every contingency.

Chapter 8

You cannot prosper doing it all by yourself

You are the key to it all but try as you may, you cannot do it all by yourself and grow at the same time. It simply cannot be done. Even a modest degree of success can suddenly overwhelm you unless you surround yourself with competent staff *and* learn how to delegate. The buzz of excitement that accompanies the outset of an enterprise can quickly turn into anxiety if you have no able lieutenants at your side to take over those tasks that you no longer have the time or personal capacity to undertake.

We have already discussed how to go about finding and keeping staff. Now let's turn our attention to the equally vital matter of delegation.

YES, YOU *CAN* DELEGATE

Most of the reasons people have for not delegating arise out of knee-jerk reactions, which have nothing to do with the tasks or the people available. Some business owners will not delegate because they are afraid. They are afraid they will lose control or that others will make mistakes. If you dump work on an employee with no explanations or expectations, instead of delegating, the worst might happen. Here are some simple steps to learn how to successfully delegate.

- **Pick the right person for the job** - Choose your people wisely. If they don't have the required skill initially, you may have to train. Be sure they have the time and the aptitude and that the new task fits in with the rest of their duties.

- **Be very clear about your expectations and have the employee repeat them back to you -** Do not dump a job on someone and run. Take the time upfront to clarify details. You want it in draft first? Double-spaced? Say so. Have the employee tell you back what you expect. We are dealing with comfort zones here. Say something like 'I am new to this delegation stuff so for my comfort, please tell me what I need you to do. It has nothing to do with my trust in your ability. I just want to be sure I explained it clearly enough.'
- **Be very clear about due dates. Determine benchmark checkpoints and write them in your calendar -** This is critical. If this is the first time you are delegating this type of project include extra dates to check on progress. Both you and the person to whom you are delegating need to record these dates. You are only checking up and advising, not hovering or taking back. Be sure to follow up on these dates.
- **Secure their commitment and assure them of your faith in their ability to do the job -** Don't assume they will do the job; ask. Don't assume they know you think they can do it, tell them.
- **Let them do it their way; different does not mean wrong -** This might be the toughest thing you will have to do. People approach projects differently. Since you have been clear with your expectations

and established follow up dates, you should be free from disaster. Let them do it their way.
- **Celebrate success** - Once the job is complete, praise people. Let them know how much they helped you and how much you appreciate their work. This is one of the best tools in a manager's arsenal. It makes people want to do more for you. And it's free.
- **Delegate more complex tasks as your confidence grows** - Give your people as much responsibility as they can handle. They'll love it and so will you.

DELEGATION ALLOWS YOU TO EXPAND YOUR OWN CAPABILITIES

You will discover that as you delegate more and more, you are able to take on more and more yourself. Freedom from routine matters frees your time to manage the enterprise creatively as opposed to running it like a clockwork motor. This is how to grow and prosper without driving yourself into the ground. It is also the way to build trust and loyalty, and to establish who your future stars are.

FACTUAL EXPERIENCE

I've always operated a 'helping hands' policy with employees. My door is always open to any member of staff and I expect my section leaders to advance the same courtesy, that way everyone is helping everyone else all of the time. Moreover, I insist on first name terms all round because you can't run a happy ship with a few of the crew tagged 'Chief' and the remainder 'Stoker'. This has never resulted in disrespect. On the contrary, it breeds deeper respect, one for the other.

Every Monday morning we take one half hour out on corporate training with each member of the team allocated thirty seconds to suggest improvements to team working. Thirty seconds isn't much, but you might be surprised at what you get out of it over a period of time.

HELPFUL HINT

Always be on the lookout for bright, trustworthy young people whom you can mould in your own image. Instil in them the philosophy of the enterprise and freely impart your own secrets for success. Do this and you will generate a conveyor belt of imaginative talents to accelerate progress by dint of youthful energy and enthusiasm. While you will lose a few along the way, you will continue to roll out your own particular brand of achievers.

Chapter 9

Cashing in on someone else's grey hairs

Why would you want to shell out hard earned cash to some old duffer to call in on you now and again and tell you where you're going wrong? Well, you wouldn't. That is not how it works, cashing in on someone else's grey hairs means taking on board the services of an elder statesperson to provide an objective overview on your undertakings. Small businesses tend to expand faster when there is someone around with a few grey hairs to cast an experienced eye occasionally on overall activity.

WHAT TO LOOK FOR IN SELECTING A PART-TIME 'MASTERMIND'

Naturally you'll want to be assured of a candidate's suitability, but before you go taking out references, here are some points to consider. You should be looking for...

- Someone with a quantifiable track record in industry or commerce - but not necessarily in the sector in which you operate.
- Someone you would find comfortable in confiding in.
- Someone with a quick grasp on disparate aspects of commercial activity.

- Someone who listens, observes, and is qualified to render objective overviews.

WHERE YOU WOULD FIND AN ELDER STATESPERSON

This is a matter of personal choice but you have options at your command.

- **Look around your circle of acquaintances** to determine whether you can identify your elder statesperson. This is by far the safest route. Someone who perhaps owned their own business and is now retired; someone who held a senior executive position in industry or commerce; someone whose expertise you admired when they were strutting their own stuff.
- **Visit your local Enterprise Trust, Enterprise Council or Small Business Bureau.** These public sector entities invariably hold on file the names and qualifications of retired senior executives who have expressed an interest in providing a service. This is also a safe route inasmuch as these bodies frequently use the services of those on the list and are therefore in a position to make qualified recommendations.
- **Place an ad in your local newspaper** and see what comes up…

HOW MUCH SHOULD YOU EXPECT TO PAY?

That varies according to status and involvement. If you are sufficiently impressed with the credentials you might want to appoint your chosen candidate in one of three ways.

- Executive director
- Part-time consultant
- Ad hoc basis on selected assignments

Alternatively, you might just strike lucky (as I did) and find yourself a mastermind for free.

FACTUAL EXPERIENCE

I am very fortunate that early in my career I met my elder statesperson mastermind (although he had no grey hairs then and still doesn't have any now). He was never directly associated with any of my enterprises; he was someone with whom I did business.

His profession was that of 'company doctor' and I have never known anyone more qualified to impart wisdom on commercial matters, and no one more gratuitous in dispensing it. We first met briefly several years beforehand on a minor project but our second meeting was conducted under the most trying of circumstances. He had been appointed chief executive of an ailing consumer electronics retail concern for which the company I was working for handled the advertising account. His remit was to resuscitate the company's fortunes and the occasion was the agency presentation on marketing recommendations for the next twelve months. He listened attentively until midway through the proceedings when he said, 'I don't wish to be unkind but - ' at which he was extremely unkind and threw out all of my senior colleagues' offerings with succinct observations on his perceived short falls in the recommendations.

Suddenly he turned to me and said, 'You ought to know what I want,' and this despite the fact that I hadn't so far made any contribution to the discussion.

We met again and alone several days later, quickly struck up a working rapport which enabled the agency to get a foot back in the door and re-present to everyone's satisfaction.

Over the years and in disparate scenarios we worked together on many assignments where he was the client and I was the supplier in principle. I could always turn to him for advice in times of stress and difficulty because I knew he had seen it all before, no matter the problem.

His name is Len Govier and he's still around, still doing business, and still as sharp as a tack. If you haven't already got a mastermind on board, go out and find yourself a Len Govier.

You'll never have cause for regret.

HELPFUL HINT

Some small business owners shy away from the notion of engaging the services of an elder statesperson, regarding the concept as unnecessary infiltration into their private affairs. I take the opposite point of view. Very often we become so immersed in our day-to-day dealings that the narrowed focus fails to pick up on both opportunity and danger signals. An experienced, impartial eye can prove a valuable counterbalance to our own committed involvement.

Chapter 10

Pick yourself up and start all over again

You will never truly appreciate success in real terms until you suffer the odd reverse or two, and when that happens, you just pick yourself up and start all over again because you cannot fail at anything until you give up.

Giving up is giving in and that is a scenario you should never even contemplate, let alone pursue.

Losers quit, winners persist - and very often persist when everyone else around is advising them to pack it in and find a job.

To have a business go under on you is not a crime and it is not failure.

You have just found another way not to do it and what you have learned from the experience (hurtful though it may be at the time) you should use as a learning curve in your next attempt at success.

The late Mike Todd, producer of the epic film *Around the World in 80 Days*, suffered frequent reversals of fortune in his brief but eventful career. He went from rags to riches several times but he still kept fighting back and when he died suddenly in the middle of a new project, his estate amounted to millions of dollars.

In an interview shortly before his untimely death he is quoted as stating,

"I've been broke many times but I have never been poor"

Poverty is a state of mind but to be impecunious as a result of a business mishap is nothing more than a state of temporary financial embarrassment. Never let impecuniousness deter you in your quest for fulfilment. It's only a by-product of a commodity: the monetary system.

As for giving up completely, listen to what Sir Winston Churchill had to say on the matter. He attended school at Harrow where he was in the lower third of his class and showed no particular potential. After he graduated he went on to university and eventually became a famous politician, a world leader, and an exceptional motivator when everyone else around him appeared to be losing the plot. Near the end of his life he was invited back to Harrow to address the student body and was introduced as one of the greatest orators of all time. The students were advised to take plenty of notes.

When Sir Winston addressed the boys he simply said,

"Young gentlemen, never give up. Never give up. Never give up. Never, never, never, never give up".

That was his entire address.

PROPER PLANNING IS THE KEY

Several years ago Tom Hunter sold his sportswear retail empire for in excess of £40million but his entrepreneurial venturing started off with disastrous results. Here is what happened in Tom's own words.

> *"Business is no picnic. You need to spend time on planning. The more you plan, the less likely it is you will fail. If you have a well thought out idea, a clear market, the*

right pricing strategy and a great team of people, then you have every chance of succeeding.

One of my heroes was Sir Jackie Stewart. So I started a go-carting business and Jackie came along to launch the venture. A few troubled months later I closed the business - I had committed the cardinal business sin by allowing my heart to rule my head. I did not research the market to see if there was a demand and I didn't pull together a cash flow forecast. I failed because I did not plan properly"

Tom Hunter did not fail. On the contrary, he dissected the cause of his initial reversal and proceeded to lay down plans for a new enterprise, which was to provide him with a fortune, much of which he has since re-invested in a series of profitable new enterprises.

WHY YOU SHOULD NEVER CONSIDER GIVING UP

Not everyone gets it right first time; some fail several times before they strike the core formula that does it for them. So, if you are failing, go ahead and fail.

But fail fast and learn from the experience.

Then try again with this new wisdom. Never give up and never suffer either.

FACTUAL EXPERIENCE

I too have suffered the pain of business reversal on more than one occasion but I have never been tempted to jack it all in and withdraw from the steaming marketplace; bloodied but unbowed sums it up. When a business proposition goes pear-shaped, you tend to take time out to lick your wounds and then suddenly something new and exciting crops up to recharge the batteries and get the adrenaline back on track.

I once had a business that I loved but it was struggling; struggling from the day the doors first opened. Like Tom Hunter I had allowed my heart to rule my head but unlike Tom, it took me rather longer to accept that it was going nowhere. My dalliance cost me dearly until one day I bit the bullet and abruptly shut up shop.

Then I picked myself up, dusted myself off, and started all over again.

HELPFUL HINT

Plan ahead and pre-test every conceivable aspect of your future undertakings and the chances are high that you will never have to pick yourself up, dust yourself off, and start all over again. Just remember though that there is no disgrace in taking the occasional tumble.

PART 2
MAINTAINING PROGRESS WITH MASTERMIND STRATEGIES

Chapter 11

Actualising self-confidence breaks down barriers

To develop confidence in handling business affairs, act confidently. Keep on acting confidently and in time you will actualise self-confidence of such magnitude that it will have the power to break down the strongest of barriers in the vital matter of minding your own business.

Self-confidence is an attitude that allows successful operators to retain positive yet realistic views of the commercial situations they face day in, day out. They trust in their own abilities, they have a general sense of control in their lives, and believe that, within reason, they will be able to achieve whatever they wish, plan, and expect.

Having self-confidence does not mean however that you will be able to do everything all by yourself. Your expectations must be realistic and when some of them fail to materialize; you must continue to be positive and to accept negative outcomes.

People who are not self-confident depend excessively on the approval of others in order to feel good about *themselves*. They tend to avoid taking risks because they fear failure. They generally do not expect to be successful. They often put themselves down and tend to discount or ignore compliments paid to them. By contrast, self-confident people are willing to risk the disapproval of others because they trust their own abilities.

They don't feel they have to conform in order to be accepted.

ASSUMPTIONS HAVE AN INFLUENCE ON SELF-CONFIDENCE

In our response to external influences, we are all guilty of developing assumptions; some of which are constructive, some harmful. Here are several that can interfere with self-confidence and some alternative ways of thinking:

- **Assumption:** *"I feel I need to obtain the approval of everyone else involved in a particular project before I can proceed with confidence"*
- **Alternative:** This is an unattainable goal. Experience tells us that it is much more realistic and desirable to develop personal standards and values that are not completely dependent on the approval of others.
- **Assumption:** *"Success in everything I undertake in business is vital to my well being"*
- **Alternative:** This is perfectionism and suggests that personal worth is always determined by achievement. Achievement can be satisfying but does not increase your self-worth. Instead, worth is an inherent quality and everyone possesses it.
- **Assumption:** *"Past influences continue to control how I react in troublesome situations"*
- **Alternative:** While it is true that confidence is especially vulnerable to external influences during the early years as a business operator, as you grow more experienced you gain awareness and perspective on what those influences represent. In so doing, you can choose which influences you will continue to allow

having an effect on your commercial life. You don't have to be helpless in the face of past events.

THE DANGER OF SELF-DEFEATING THOUGHT PATTERNS

Subscribing to harmful assumptions leaves you vulnerable to self-defeating thought patterns:

- **All-or-nothing syndrome.** *"I feel like a total failure when my performance is less than perfect"*. This is a surefire strategy for screwing things up big time.
- **Seeing only dark clouds.** *"Disaster lurks around every corner and comes to be expected"*. For example, a single negative detail, piece of criticism, or passing comment darkens reality and sets off alarm bells.
- **Magnifying the negative/minimising the positive.** *"Winning doesn't count nearly as much as losing. I bagged three deals in a row but losing out on this one makes me feel terrible about myself"*. This has to be the ultimate in negative thinking.
- **Uncritical acceptance of emotions as truth.** *"I feel inadequate so it must be true"*. So no one remarked today how great you are, so what?
- **Overemphasis on 'should' statements.** 'Should' statements are invariably reflective of the expectations of other people rather than expressive of your own wants and desires. *'I should have listened to Fred, and then I wouldn't have blown it.'* Dependence on the opinion of others is a self-defeating pursuit.
- **Labelling.** A simplistic process that often conveys a sense of blame.

"I am a loser and it's all my fault." Never put labels on yourself. They have a habit of doing exactly what you say they will do.
- **Difficulty in accepting compliments.** *"Do you really think I did okay in that presentation? I thought I was bottling it towards the end".* Do this and you are inviting acquiescence.

STRATEGIES FOR DEVELOPING SELF-CONFIDENCE

- **Emphasize your strengths.** Give yourself credit for everything you try. By focusing on what you can do, you applaud yourself for effort rather than emphasising end product. Starting from a base of what you do well helps you to live within the bounds of your inevitable limitations.
- **Take risks.** Approach new experiences as opportunities to learn rather than occasions to win or lose. Doing so opens you up to new possibilities and can increase your sense of self-acceptance. Not doing so turns every possibility into an opportunity for failure, and inhibits personal growth.
- **Use self-talk.** Use self-talk as an opportunity to counter harmful assumptions. Then tell yourself to bin unreality and substitute more acceptable assumptions. For example: when you catch yourself expecting perfection, be aware that you can't do everything perfectly, that it's only possible to do things as well as you can. This allows you to accept yourself as you are while still striving to improve.
- **Self-evaluate.** Learn to evaluate yourself independently. Doing so allows you to avoid the constant

sense of turmoil that comes from relying exclusively on the opinions of others. Focusing internally on how you feel about your own commercial performance will give you a stronger sense of self and will prevent you from giving your personal power away too easily to others.

FACTUAL EXPERIENCE

Many years ago when I was operating as regional director for a national advertising agency group, I had thrust upon me a scenario that called for the immediate actualisation of confidence in my own abilities. There was an alternative. I could simply walk away and watch the group (together with my modest but valuable shareholding) suffer an almost certain terminal loss. The client in question was the electronics giant Philips and the villain of the piece was the agency account director who had locked himself away in his bedroom at home feigning a nervous breakdown. He was refusing to speak to anyone, including his wife.

The urgent call for my services came from the group chairman and the problem was gargantuan. Some five months previously Philips had issued the miscreant account director with a 36-page brief on the matter of the agency presenting its marketing recommendations on the rationalisation and re-launch under a single banner of 400 UK based consumer electronics retail stores. Currently there were 27 different trading names and 27 disparate marketing policies. The presentation in Eindhoven was now just four days away. The original brief could not be located, the account director wasn't taking calls, and it was unthinkable to ask the client for a copy. My chairman's remit was for me to drop everything, fly to Heathrow and take immediate control of the fiasco.

I said I would do it but on condition that should my efforts prove successful in retaining the business, I would personally handle the account forthwith. He agreed without hesitation.

What met me at the crisis meeting in London that evening filled me with foreboding. The creative team were in a state of flux and no constructive strategy was forthcoming. I decided to dispense with their services, flew in one of my own creative heads on the shuttle, and set about the task in hand. Drawing upon our collective retail experience, we devised a strategy from our own hastily constructed brief, worked through two consecutive days and nights, slept through the third, and departed for Eindhoven on a wing and a prayer on the morning of the fourth day.

The presentation was conducted in chilling silence before a battery of Philips executives. At the conclusion the director of retail operations thanked us both for our contribution, enquired as to where we were located, and announced that he would visit our offices at ten o'clock the following morning with his verdict.

True to his word he turned up right on time and after the briefest of meetings, confirmed that the agency had retained the business - but on condition that it be handled out of our provincial premises. The account was worth £500,000, a massive budget thirty years ago.

The actualisation of collective self-confidence had succeeded in winning over the client's trust despite the extremely grave scenario.

HELPFUL HINT

Positive thinking coupled with steadfast refusal to kowtow to outside influences is the key to actualising self-confidence.

Listen to what others have to say by all means, evaluate their offerings, and then take your own counsel before proceeding in your deliberations.

Chapter 12

Decisiveness: the key to achievement

There are two age-old adages proffering cold comfort when facing difficult decisions.

1. When in doubt, do nothing
2. To decide not to decide is also a decision

Such statements are dangerous because they advocate procrastination, the thief of time, the destroyer of ambition. Decisiveness is the key to achievement, as William Shakespeare succinctly encapsulates in his famous one-liner,

'T'were done, t'were best done now'

Every day we face challenges in our business dealings, situations obliging us to make a decision, one way or the other. Most of these are simplistic and the response automatic. Others though are more problematic and call for painstaking introspection. Analysis is good, essential more often than not, but avoid over-analysing the situation. That invites your mind to consider doubt followed by procrastination, leaving you wide open to missing out on a solution or an opportunity.

Analyse, decide; then act. There may be risks involved in your calculation but they will far outweigh those that infest procrastination.

WHEN INSTANT DECISIONS ARE REQUIRED

On occasion the problem will be so serious and so time sensitive that you are required to act not only decisively, but swiftly, implementing strategies that have the power to restructure a business, catapult it to outstanding success or kill it stone dead, should the measures taken prove to be unsound. You will draw upon your inner reserve of native attributes (you have them in abundance or you wouldn't be in business on your own account), face up squarely to the crisis, formulate a plan, and act upon it decisively. Crucial matters such as the sudden drying up of essential supplies, cash running out, or treachery within your ranks don't hang about awaiting a solution. They have to be dealt with instantly or they spread like a cancer.

HOW TO HANDLE THE INTROSPECTION PROCESS

- **Identify the warning signals**. How, where, when and why did they come to light? Have you missed any others that might have a bearing on the eventual outcome? What the ear doesn't hear, the eye cannot visualise - so listen, observe and analyse.
- **Evaluate the situation**. Do it calmly but with a sense of urgency, using this strategy for swift and decisive evaluation. Take a sheet of A4, draw a line down the

middle, put a 'plus' at the top of one side, a 'minus' at the other. If you end up with no plusses, you have a real problem on your hands.
- **Analyse the risks**. Do this conscientiously even if it scares the hell out of you - but don't start yet on searching for solutions.
- **Discriminate between types of risk**. Not every risk results in the same outcome. Review your analysis and scale the risks in order of gravity.
- **Devise risk strategies**. Now you can start looking for solutions. Devise a series of remedial strategies starting with the most serious risk on your list.
- **Avoid analysis paralysis**. Accomplish all of the foregoing rationally and rapidly; leaving emotion out of the equation (you can handle the demons later). Above all, resist the temptation to cover the same ground over and over again or you will contract analysis paralysis and end up in total frustration.
- **Discuss your findings with others only if you must**. If you are a one-man operation, keep your findings to yourself for now. If you have partners or co-directors you may be obliged to open up but restrain anyone from pressing the red alert.
- **Take your own counsel in the final analysis**. It is your own business you are minding, so make sure that any proposed course of action is based on your own findings.

HOW TO PROCEED DECISIVELY

- **Draw up a plan for your prescribed course of remedial action**. With all the available information at your command, lock yourself away and develop

your plan to completion, even if it takes you through the night.
- **Commit to its enactment within a given time frame.** Sort out your time frames and commit yourself to action.
- **Move into action**

FACTUAL EXPERIENCE

Saatchi & Saatchi bought the agency group outright and for a while it was all wine and roses. I got a handsome return on my modest shareholding and as an added bonus my end of the company was restyled Saatchi Green. The honeymoon was soon over though when I discovered that while I worked well with the new owners up to the point of purchase, I was most uncomfortable working *for* them. It wasn't their fault, it was mine: I never was much good at reporting.

This feeling of uneasiness intensified when I discovered some six months later that they were secretly negotiating to buy another similar size ad agency and merge it with mine. Now where would I be? Further down the pecking order was a possibility and out of it all together was another. I decided to cut loose and start all over again.

It was a considerable undertaking with enormous risks attached, but one I had to take to regain peace of mind and preserve my standing in a highly competitive industry. The plans were laid and while money would be tight I had no need of external funding. What I did need though was to convince the clientele that this extraordinary development would be to their long-term advantage.

This I managed to achieve from 100 per cent of the client base (they were all *my* customers) following a series of clandestine meetings. The rest of the plan had to be completed quietly and quickly, and it was. Within one week I had formed a limited company, signed a lease on new premises, persuaded the staff to tender their resignations en masse and then issued them with contracts to work for my new concern.

Then I told Saatchi.

The speed of my defection took them by surprise and left the management vulnerable in their negotiations to purchase the other agency. Sparks flew, threats were issued, and then the breakaway was turned on its head within twenty-four hours. Saatchi suggested a management buyout and for a nominal sum I purchased the goodwill of the now defunct operation.

You might reasonably argue that all of this was treachery on my part, and perhaps to an extent it was, but neither CEO Tim (Lord) Bell nor I saw it that way. We both knew the marriage was doomed.

HELPFUL HINT

Indecision begets undesirable states of mind such as frustration, anxiety and worry, which invariably results in exacerbating the situation. When faced with problematic scenarios in your business affairs follow the clear-cut guidelines listed in this chapter and then move into decisive action.

Chapter 13

Devising a strategy for every situation

To win more often than you lose in the world of commerce, you will require to develop the knack of devising strategies for every type of situation; the good, the bad, the indifferent. There is nothing difficult about this. Start off by undertaking the exercise outlined in the previous chapter. Take a sheet of A4; adjust the sequence of instructions to your particular requirements, then crack on devising strategies. Practice the technique and you will be rewarded by the labyrinth of your subconscious providing you with a steady stream of viable strategies for every type of problematic situation or avenue of opportunity associated with your operation.

You could try it another way of course by steeping yourself in academe. You won't be stuck for choice.

Thousands of articles and hundreds of books have been published on the subject of *strategy*; strategic planning, strategic marketing, strategic overviews, strategic this, strategic that, strategic the other. But they all relate to the same premise; the ability to think on your feet. Read such tomes by all means (if you have the time or the inclination) but be selective and always remember that the only real masters of the business arts are the ones who are actually out there doing it, day in, day out. What they have learned in the hard school of knocks says it all:

Strategy = Planing = Resolution

WHY MOST START UPS FLOUNDER AND GO UNDER

It is well documented that the failure rate for new business propositions of every description is extremely high in the early years of trading. This is not by coincidence, bad luck or happenstance; it is underpinned by a unifying factor. Start ups that set sail in a sea of excitement, then flounder and go under, invariably do so because they discard the very compass that will guide them safely from port to port in their quest for survival, yet alone success. The devising of this compass was their initial act in the art of strategy making, and yet it is usually the first piece of equipment to be jettisoned.

The business plan
Those who refer to it every working day, revise it, refine it, are all the time developing a strategy for lifelong success. Those who use it once for funding and then consign it to gather dust on a shelf are developing a strategy for imminent failure.

And there are no exceptions, no exemptions.

Pop music, for example, is just as much an industry as any other you can think of, so why then are there so many one-hit wonders? Is it because the participants have no talent or because they're working with rubbish material? I doubt it, because they have already evidenced a degree of competence through early albeit transient success. Those few who make the grade and manage to capitalise on initial attainment do so because they have a strategy for the future, a plan of action for fulfilment. The many that fall at the first hurdle are invariably represented by management that has neither the experience nor the wit to develop winning strategies.

EVERYDAY STRATEGIES FOR PERSONAL DEVELOPMENT

You can also pull down ready-made strategies any time you like, strategies to put into practice at will to further personal development and enhance aptitude. For example:

- **Make something happen.** Make initiative your target for next week. Taking the initiative doesn't mean being pushy, obnoxious, or aggressive. It means recognising your responsibility to make things happen. If you want to motivate your staff express that motivation through action. If you want to increase sales, lower overheads, or solve a vexing operational problem, take the initiative and make something happen.

- **Increase your visibility.** Leaders can be quietly competent, but they must be visible. Your task is to work side by side with one of your front-line employees for at least a half a day. Discover what it's like to work in the factory, or to sit on the phone fielding vexatious customer service calls. By participating you'll convey that no one is above doing the work that needs to be done. Be bold, and do the work with gusto even if you've never done it before. Be visible. The word will get around.

- **Look for trouble.** Take on a tough assignment. Show your followers that you're willing to tackle their problems hands on.

STRATEGIC PLANNING FOR OPPORTUNITY

When opportunity comes knocking at your door (it does so many times) you will want to be in a position to take full advantage, and the best way to achieve a state of readiness is to be constantly honing up your skills on strategy making. The more you practice, the better prepared you will be to handle any challenge.

When you get the call, some healthy self-talk and your A4 sheet will come in handy. Let's assume you are the owner operator of a small graphics house and out of the blue you are invited to pitch for a sizeable chunk of new business. There is a comprehensive brief attached to the invitation and it specifies the requirement for a full-scale presentation. There is also an offer from the prospective client of further clarification on any aspect(s) of the brief. Be on the safe side and take them up on that before committing hefty expenditure to this 'wonderful' opportunity.

Enter stage right: your sheet of A4…

On the up side
1. This is a prestigious account. Winning it will lift us right up there among the big boys.

2. We must come highly recommended.

3. Adrenaline is running on high in the studio - best get the presentation online straightaway.

4. We'll recover the presentation costs by amortising them across future work.

5. We stand to make a lot of money.

On the down side

1. Or is it yet another 'cattle call'? And have you been brought in just to make up the numbers?

2. Oh really? Check that out. There are lots of Machiavellian people out there.

1. Hold up. There's no mention of a presentation fee in the brief.

2. This is a fee-based account remember. They'll spot recovery of costs a mile away.

3. Look again at the fee base. Will there be irrecoverable costs over and above?

Conclusion
- Request an early meeting with the prospective client
- Tie up loose ends before committing to presentation

Action
- Ask for a complete list of the contenders

- Ask why invitation was rendered
- Ask did it come by way of recommendation
- Ask for a presentation fee
- Ask for a complete analysis of the fee based payment structure

Subsequent action
- If no presentation fee is forthcoming, decide whether to proceed
- If proceeding, trim costs accordingly

FACTUAL EXPERIENCE

I was operating a marketing services consultancy at the time of the last but one reorganisation of local government in the United Kingdom when I was approached to present recommendations on the launch of a newly designated council: Strathclyde Region. Briefing particulars were conspicuous by their absence, so I requested an early meeting with the acting public relations official with whom I had worked on several assignments for the City of Glasgow under the old political regime.

Although the elected members were in position and the governing policies established, there was no structure, no remit, no paid officials, and no direction. It was all still in the melting pot. The acting PR did his best to provide an outline brief but all he talked about were the policies, all of which I noted were being committed to shorthand by one of my colleagues at the meeting. We were also advised that twenty-seven (yes, 27) other consultancies had responded to a statutory advertisement announcing the opportunity and that submissions from all of them would be considered. It was heading up to be the biggest bun fight of the century.

My shorthand colleague judiciously enquired of the acting PR.

'What do you hope to achieve from this campaign?'

He replied inconclusively, 'We want to inform the populace as to what we are all about'

Back at the office I conferred with my departmental chiefs and we were of the concerted opinion that we should decline the invitation because there was no brief and we stood to lose a fortune on presentation costs as our chances of success were 27-1 against.

The lady shorthand colleague disagreed.

'But we do have a brief of sorts, the policies, which is all they know about. *And* we don't need to spend any money on the presentation. Let the others blow their money. All we need do is submit a pentel scamp'

'How do you make that out?' I asked, not unreasonably.

'Because apart from droning on about the policies, all the PR could offer was constant re-iteration of 'we're changing for the better' and 'we want to tell people what it's all about'. He doesn't know what it's all about, his masters don't know, so let's ask the people to help'

'And'

'We show them one layout for a full-page ad to be placed in every newspaper in the new region over a four-week period. The heading will be '*Change For The Better*', the body copy will consist of pockets of copy and symbolic illustrations highlighting the policies, and then we round it all off with a strap line '*We Need Your Help To Help Us To Get It Right*'.

We won the business as a direct result of one lady's ability to think on her feet, dissect seemingly vacuous information and create a winning strategy.

HELPFUL HINT

You can devise winning strategies for anything, anywhere, anytime. I often produce mine when I'm travelling; on the reverse side of airline, rail and public transport tickets. The trick is to get into the habit of churning out strategies at the drop of a hat because when you've mastered that art, no vexatious situation will ever take you unawares again.

Chapter 14

Mastering the art of providing good service

You might *just* get away for a time with marketing a substandard product, but you'll never get away at any time with providing inferior service. You'll be found out in a hundred different ways. In the bricks and mortar environment the essential elements in the provision of good service tend to vary from one industry to another, but they are all directed towards the one end: **keeping the customer happy**. No one lasts long in retailing, for example, unless time and energy are constantly expended on matters such as enhancing store lighting, improving ease of traffic flow, extending the range of options to pay, and excelling in customer care.

AVENUE OF OPPORTUNITY

The pressure is unrelenting and the demands increase in tandem with the changes in trading patterns occasioned by the phenomenal growth of information technology. And yet in this very technology lies an avenue of opportunity if we but take the time to examine it. Most small businesses nowadays have an Internet presence of sorts in the shape of a modestly constructed web site. But how many use it for the purpose the web was invented: the receipt *and* distribution of valuable information?

Your web site provides the cyberspace way to foster good customer relations and to engender loyalty by providing a constant stream of variable information on all matters relating to service.

It's called 'e-service'.

Here's how it works and you can tailor it to your own particular requirements.

EIGHT SECRETS FOR SUCCESSFUL E-SERVICE

Effective e-service, despite the apparent obstacles, is actually a very achievable goal. As numerous successful implementers have demonstrated, it simply requires the right principles, practices, and tools. Eight basic attributes make web-based customer support work for any business, no matter how small:

- **Making sure your web site 'listens' to customers** - Every successful salesperson knows the most important part of their job is listening - both for explicit and implicit messages. Web sites should do the same. Explicit messages are clear requests for specific information. Implicit messages are patterns of queries or usage that imply a lack of or difficulty in finding some type of content. An effective web presence requires mechanisms and/or practices that ensure an attentive ear to both types of online customer requirements.

- **Giving customers what they want** - It's not enough to ascertain which types of content users are asking for: the content must also be provided quickly. The atmosphere of the web is driven by a sense of immediacy. Delays in delivering customer-driven content can be deadly. An e-service solution must capture customer requests and use that information to automatically enhance site content for future visitors.

- **Responsive content and response mechanisms that are easy to find and easy to use** - It's remarkable how many web site designers allow customers to wind up in places where they can't easily find a way to ask for more information or send an email request. On many sites, the 'Contact Us' button simply launches a pre-addressed email screen - with no information about how soon they can expect a reply or where else to look for information. Many sites don't even provide a phone number if a customer really needs to talk to someone right away. If customers can't even find the company phone number, what are the chances that they will be able to find an even more obscure piece of information? **Hidden content is the same as no content at all.** Of course, this is true of all types of content, but it's especially critical for response-related pages. So e-service must be easy for customers to use.

- **Appreciating the 80/20 rule** - While it's great to make sure web site content is as comprehensive as possible, the fact remains that - on average - **80% of all site traffic is aimed at 20% of the content.** In other words, a relatively small amount of content can take care of a tremendous amount of business if it's the right content. So small businesses that delay putting up sites because they're trying to make sure they can answer every possible customer question online are making a mistake. It's much smarter to get the most important information up first, and then add to it over time as dictated by customer needs.

- **Why it pays to get pushy** - You don't have to rely on customers coming to your site to get them the information they need. **By offering a variety of email notification options, you can turn a customer's email box into an extension of your web site.** A good way to do this is to ask visitors if they would like to be notified if there is any change in a specified content area, such as a product catalogue or a press release archive. Such notify-on-change 'push' mechanisms allow you to leverage your web site and build an ongoing electronic relationship with your customers.

- **Respond quickly or risk losing the customer forever** - As highlighted in a recent major study based on consumer feedback (*Right Now Technology Study, 2002*) many businesses make the mistake of being too slow in their response to online information requests. **Once a customer or prospect has been disappointed by how slowly their question has been answered, they are unlikely to try again.** They might even become disillusioned about the operation as a whole. If you're going to offer even a bare bones email contact mechanism, make sure it results in a fast reply - preferably as early as possible on the following working day.

- **Track for information as it comes in** - Because a large percentage of site visitors tend to have the same narrow set of questions, it's critically important to track requests for information as they come in. Consistent tracking of requests allows those in charge of site content to determine where to direct their efforts

- allowing for much more efficient use of resources. Effective e-service applications perform this tracking automatically and dynamically rank information based on historical usefulness to customers. This 'sameness' in questions is all the more reason to include a **FAQ** (frequently asked questions) section on the Web site.

- **Automate, automate, automate** - All the tasks required to create a truly responsive site - assimilating and analysing user queries, developing appropriate content and posting it in a well-organised manner, handling ad hoc and 'push' email communications, etc. - can be extremely labour-intensive. As site traffic increases, these tasks can pile up even more. **Many sites are spoiled by their own success, as the volume of communications exceeds the resources dedicated to supporting that communication.** So, it is critically important to deploy effective automation tools that can scale to meet rising demands. Such tools significantly increase the return on staff and infrastructure resources invested in the web. Good e-service applications automate site maintenance tasks and eliminate time-consuming knowledge collection and engineering functions - functions that, when neglected over time, result in out-of-date content and dissatisfied customers.

These simple procedures can make the difference between online success and online failure. As so many operations continue to demonstrate, online success not only has an impact on how a company is perceived by its customers, but also on how it is perceived by Internet users en masse.

Visit www.rightnowtechnologies.com for a comprehensive review on all matters relating to the successful implementation of your own e-service facility.

SURVEY YOUR WEB SITE VISITORS

A good way to kick off your e-service project is to set up a simple 'feedback' form. Asking for feedback from visitors to your site is one of the best ways to obtain suggestions about improving your merchandise—and an online survey is a fast, convenient and inexpensive method to gather information, including:

- What do your customers and prospects want to buy?
- How do they like your current product or service?
- How would they improve it?
- What do they think of your competition?

Always respond quickly with a 'thank-you' email for their participation. This helps create a bond that keeps customers and converts prospects.

FACTUAL EXPERIENCE

Until the incidence and rapid growth of the Internet, authors found it virtually impossible to *create* let alone maintain contact with their readers. Now they are able to do this effortlessly and automatically. In my own writing activities (and in common with an ever-increasing number of authors) I operate several multi-page information web sites where I provide my readers with a variety of channels for news and contact:

- **Home Page** - with the focus on my latest work
- **Bibliography** - listing all published titles
- **Services** - information on my availability for lecturing, book reviewing, etc.
- **Guest Page** - where readers can log in and record comments
- **Contact** - providing my personal email address
- **Ezine** - where they can subscribe to my free newsletter

Give some serious thought to the final entry. With your own free **newsletter** on offer, you will pick up a steady stream of email addresses from which you can build up a valuable targeted mailing list.

HELPFUL HINT

You won't win any prizes for providing good service but you will go bust very quickly if you don't. Make customer servicing a priority and always be on the lookout for imaginative new channels for its provision.

Chapter 15
The amazing power of words in minding your own business

Communication is the universal platform on which all business is conducted.

And yet, how often we take for granted the very instruments that constitute the basis of our ability to communicate effectively. Words; they have the power to inspire or depress, the power to evoke acceptance or rejection, the power to clinch or lose a deal, the power to make or break a business.

Diction - What you say and how you say it are of equal importance. Always choose your words carefully, and never use a word where you are uncertain of the *precise* meaning. It could rebound on you, creating an outcome you'd rather not have.

Correspondence - Every written communication you issue is an ambassador for your enterprise, be it directed to customers, suppliers or employees. Never dispatch anything until it has been thoroughly checked for accuracy of structure, content and syntax. Mistakes jar, they stick, and they reflect badly on professionalism.

Telephone - Even the smallest concern needs telephonic communication for sales, service, ordering, collecting dues, etc. It is good business practice to ensure that everyone in the organisation follows a set pattern for making and responding to calls.

Marketing - Advertising, marketing, promotion all depend heavily on the amazing power of words to get the message across. A superbly crafted illustration might paint a thousand words in realms of art appreciation, but in the context of hard tack marketing your super-duper graphics won't get you very far unless they are accompanied by compelling, persuasive dialogue.

Selling - When you are walking the talk in a face-to-face sales pitch, it isn't your beloved product or service that wins the day; it is your powers of expression. Prospects aren't there to be sold to, but they will willingly buy from you if they like what you have to say, and how you say it. This is not to imply that he/she who barks loudest in the marketplace always brings home the bacon. On the contrary, the best presenters are invariably quiet, introspective individuals who have a firm grasp on the essential tenets of word power and who know instinctively how to put the message across to best effect.

Internet - People the world over use the Internet to source information. They choose a search engine, insert a word or several key words, which in turn leads them to more words and so on until they have compiled a catalogue of data on what they want to know. So, when are setting out to create your own commercial presence on the Internet, make words your prime priority. Words are what cyberspace is all about. Web creation tools, graphics, sound, animation, gizmos are all available to be downloaded for free, but the words - the most essential ingredient - are all down to you. Make sure you spend the bulk of your time on their composition before you tackle the packaging.

PUTTING THE MAGIC OF WORDS TO WORK IN YOUR BUSINESS

Having established the amazing effect that words have on every aspect of doing business, let's now look at just a few ways to put this magic to work in your business. The examples provided are equally adaptable to general correspondence, advertising, promotion, email marketing, web page copy, etc.

Certain words are irresistible - Certain words, when combined together, literally draw the reader's eyes to your message. The paired words below are those that experienced copywriters claim work every time.

You / Ultimate - **Free** / Master - **Power** / Discovery - **Easy** / Guaranteed - **Love** / Money **New** / Scientific - **Proven** / Results - **Incredible** / Discovery - **Breakthrough** / Secret - **Private** / Cash - **Shocked** / Shocking - **Revealed** / Uncovered - **Hidden** / Profits **Inside** / Sale

Power words, like those above, are already **implanted deeply** in the minds of all of us simply because of what the words **mean**. For example, when your author and most everyone else sees the word **Discovery**, it evokes a response from within and draws attention to the rest of the sentence because Discovery '**means**' something to me and to most other people. The Discovery might give me a great **advantage** before you and others find out if I read about it first. People love to discover things and the word **attracts** them

Why bulleted benefit lists create buyers - Bulleting the benefits (*not features*) of your product or service works best because it allows the prospect to encapsulate at a glance what your offer is about. Bullet lists are applicable in any promotional context but they work particularly well in Internet marketing because they help prevent users bounding from your site to another without reading at least some of the content. Bullet the benefits and you will stop them in their tracks.

Review your product in detail, extract every possible benefit someone would get from it and write them all down. Do this before you even attempt to compose the actual sales copy. You will find by doing so that the benefit list you're writing will make your own mind explode with creative ideas and the sales pitch will literally write itself from there on.

Benefit lists make it very clear what the reader gets. Since the reader is only concerned with what he/she gets, benefit lists are your most powerful sales weapons.

Here's an example benefit list from a money-making book by Alan Says, founder of the famous *Internet Marketing Warriors* educational programme

- **How to create** your own **150** page book in **8** days or less
- **Combine** the **Internet** and **fax-on-demand** for **unstoppable** profits
- **Create** your own **e-book** in less than **2 minutes**
- **Add** this '**one**' line to your site and say **goodbye** to your competition
- **Master** the art of **sales letter writing** by reading the **Magic Book**

- **Control** how your **prospects** see you with this **simple** strategy

To make your own bulleted benefits list, review your product or service in detail. The more benefits you come up with the better

- *Headlines - the ad for the ad -* Your sales message may be incredible, but if your headline doesn't catch them the message will never get read. You must understand the power and importance of headlines. 80 per cent of the power and effectiveness of your ad is in the headline you choose. One will have the power to draw the reader into the body of your message and another will not. You must test. One headline will pull up to 1500 per cent more response/profit than another will. For example, ebooks that sold few copies became bestsellers when the publisher stripped the title (headline) and replaced it with another. The rest of the book remained exactly the same. Powerful headlines must scream out the biggest benefits you can think of. They must grab prospects and entice them to read more.

- *Using subheads to catch quick readers -* Break up your copy with exciting subheads. Subheads catch the 'skimmers' and entice them into the body of your message. Many people skim over page after page fast. They do it even faster on the Internet. If you have powerful subheads throughout your marketing blurb, one or more of them will catch these skimmers and draw them in. Create your subheads just like you do your main headline.

- ***Educate, inform and sell more*** - Educate the readers of your sales message. Give them some knowledge, some inside information that they didn't know before and you are a hundred times more likely to make the sale. When the reader learns something from you, it adds tremendous credibility to your message. It gives a very powerful sense of realness about you and your company. Trust is established and the beginnings of a positive relationship. This is worth more than gold.

FACTUAL EXPERIENCE

I once lost out on a pitch for a valuable piece of new business and it made me wonder why. My consultancy had a good working relationship with the client in question and we had in fact pulled them out of the fire on more than one occasion on tight schedule one-off projects. All the more reason, I though, we should have won the business. I decided to find out why not and telephoned the client marketing director.

Having expressed my disappointment at the outcome of the pitch, he handed me a document and replied, 'Perhaps when you read this, you will understand'

The document was in fact the report submitted by the winning contender. It contained no more than a dozen pages, which included the presentation graphics.

As I read the report I appreciated why we had been unsuccessful. It was a masterpiece of brevity and clarity and where we had used several paragraphs to illustrate a point; it used a single sentence. It demonstrated **concisely** that not only did the author understand the client brief, but equally concisely demonstrated how it would be fulfilled.

I had learned a valuable lesson inasmuch as quantity does not necessarily equate quality. We had submitted a 50-page report plus mounds of individual graphics. Perhaps we overawed the client; perhaps we simply bored them.

Whatever, from that day on I have always treated the amazing power of words with the utmost respect in minding my own business.

HELPFUL HINT

Consider for a moment living in a world without words or operating a business without communication. It is inconceivable. Yet how often do we take the power of words for granted; a power that can be ephemeral or everlasting at our discretion. Delivered thoughtlessly, words have a short-lived impact; delivered painstakingly, they have the power to open closed doors. Treat the words you utter or commit to print with the utmost respect and you will prosper in your business dealings.

Chapter 16

Developing your own distinctive style

"Style, when you've got it, you stand out a mile"
—*Frank Sinatra*

And he would know. His own very distinctive style of singing captured the hearts of teenage bobbysoxers at the outset of the 1940s. But he didn't stop there. He proceeded to develop his special style to cater for changing tastes and wider audiences in a career spanning five successive decades. Music was Frank Sinatra's business, but whatever yours is, you can and should endeavour to develop your own distinctive style. Like the man said, you'll stand out a mile, and you will do that because no two people operating in the same business sector go about it in exactly the same way. Those who set their own high standards and exude flair quickly capture the heart of the marketplace.

HOW TWO BROTHERS REVOLUTIONISED AN ENTIRE INDUSTRY

When the brothers Saatchi first set up shop in the early 1970s, advertising agencies were being suffocated by their own self-importance. These two young men arrived on the scene like a breath of fresh air in a dank and moribund industry. They had some funding but no clients and in the beginning, their flamboyance was considered as little more than can rattling by the establishment. The brothers set about their mission and persuaded that doyen of public sector blue chip accounts, The Health Education Council (HEC) to embark on a series of shock treatment ad campaigns to promote vital health care issues. The results were as instant as they were astonishing: highest ever consumer attention levels and highest ever client awareness.

Soon they had the commercial sector big spenders jousting with each other to sample the Saatchi style of service, and not long after that, the commercial banks were competing to provide enormous sums of money to fund an ambitious acquisition drive. The distinctive Saatchi style had revolutionised an entire industry over a few short years.

CREATING YOUR OWN DISTINCTIVE STYLE

Few if any of us are as talented as the Saatchis but that is no reason why we should not examine how we currently conduct business to determine whether there are areas we could revitalise by adding a touch of style to our approach. Here are some aspects you might consider worthy of review.

- **Marketing** - Do you continue to use the same marketing methods year in, year out? Look around, see what's fresh, and try something new. If you use an advertising agency, spring a surprise now and then by asking them to re-pitch in competition with other agencies. That will be enough to sharpen *their* style and in the process provide you with a range of disparate approaches.

- **Sales and distribution** - Could your sales policy do with a spring clean and are you up to snuff on the changing patterns in distribution? Sometimes staying in the comfort zone can cost you dearly. Put your style to work and discover areas of opportunity you may be currently missing out on.

- **Presentation** - If your business involves presentation and demonstration, could you improve on performance by adding a little style to the proceedings? Think about it. There are lots of good books and tapes available to help you add zing and zest to your technique.

- **Buying** - Does your buying policy revolve exclusively around automatic knee jerk reactions to diminishing stock levels? Have you been out and about recently to see what's new on offer? When did you last consider adding new lines of merchandise, perhaps on a sale or return basis? Press the style button and get cracking.

- **Customer service** - Inject some style into your service strategy by being bold enough to ask customers what they really want from you. The famous bandleader Joe Loss always knew *exactly* what his customers wanted. On tours around provincial dance halls and when his musicians were taking a break, Joe forswore the coffee and elected instead to mingle and talk with the patrons, assessing their disparate tastes in popular music. That is why is the Joe Loss

Ballroom Orchestra topped the polls from the 1930s through to the end of the 1970s.

- **Collecting dues** - Style in debt collection? You bet there is. If you struggle to get the cash in on time, investigate your options on alternative ways to collect outstanding dues.

FACTUAL EXPERIENCE

Two people I had never met in my life before demonstrated inordinate style to save my clients and me from considerable embarrassment during an impasse in an important conference. The venue was Brussels and the occasion was a presentation to European advertising agents on the merits of a quality UK daily newspaper. As the guests trooped in to fill the seats in a rectangular format, the speakers (comprising senior executives from the management side) were conspicuous by their absence. I departed hastily, made some enquiries, and discovered that they'd all been on the town the previous night and were unable to stand upright let alone speak at the conference. I conferred with the senior audio-visual technician and advised him of my decision to cancel the event.

'Why?' he protested, 'You can handle it yourself'

'No, I can't. There are five different native tongues out there and I can't depend on them all understanding English'

'Do the geysers who are supposed to be here speak five languages?'

'I doubt they do. But how do we handle it?'

'No bovver guv,' he replied cheerfully. 'We'll get an interpreter down from the EEC building across the road. She'll handle the lingo; you busk it on the questions'

Reluctantly I agreed to his suggestion and within minutes an attractive young Egyptian lady appeared at my side and briefed me on how to proceed. She introduced me as the managing director of the 'quality' newspaper, cued me in on my impromptu spiel, invited and fielded questions from the audience, translated for my benefit, and even contributed on how best to answer. The whole affair went like a dream and the fiasco turned into a triumph.

These two incredible people had seen it all before, but more importantly, they had the style to see it through once more.

HELPFUL HINT

Don't make the mistake of confusing style with flamboyance. Style has no requirement to be bright and showy or make its presence felt by behaving in a noticeable, extravagant manner. More often than not, true style expresses itself in quiet, unobtrusive effectiveness. People who exude style in business invariably do so without the necessity for drawing attention to their accomplishments.

Chapter 17

Getting what you want with gentle persuasion

Persuasion is the art of getting people to do something they wouldn't ordinarily do if you didn't ask. When meeting with a prospective client for the first time, you are trying to understand their problems, determine their objectives, explain *your* services and outline the many benefits of working with you. But what if it's not going anywhere? No matter how much you ask, how well you present your advantages or how sincere you are about helping this prospective client, things don't seem to be clicking.

SELLING THE FUTURE

What I mean by this is going beyond outlining objectives, value and measures of success (which most of us don't do a good job with to begin with) and helping the prospective client get in touch with their real motivation to take action, to move in a new direction. This motivation always lies in the future and it lies inside the client, not outside. You need to go beyond the surface and discover their highest aspirations, their most compelling dreams.

HOW DO YOU DO THAT?

Once you've learned about their situation, their problems, and discussed objectives and outcomes, what you need to do now is dig deeper and learn why those solutions or outcomes are important to them. You're really always asking the same question: 'If you got X, then after you have it, what do you want that's even more important?' But as simple as this might seem, the ultimate result can be very powerful.

What happens in this process of selling the future is that **your prospects get in touch with what they really want,** what's really important to them. And when that is clear, people become motivated to move heaven and earth to get that result. If you have helped facilitate this process, they will see you as a *partner* in producing that result. You've asked the right questions, you've listened, and you have resonated with what was important to them. You've clicked.

PERSUASION AS A SELLING TOOL

In his book *Marketing Explained* Anthony Worrall claims that we should never overtly act or talk persuasively in a selling scenario - but he does not argue against *using* persuasion as a sales tactic. The only reason some salespeople use overt persuasion is because the value of what they have to offer doesn't really address the needs of the prospective client. Manipulative closes, leading questions, and other less-than-savory selling techniques should have no place in your repertoire. If you truly believe in what you have to offer and do your best to find out what's needed, you will become **gently persuasive without being pushy** in getting what you want.

IS SELLING A TALENT, A SKILL, OR A PROCESS?

Selling is all of the above, and if you're going to be successful in your small business you've got to first understand sales technique and then master it. There are many misconceptions about the art of selling: 'Sales is about deception'; 'Sales means being pushy'; 'Sales is manipulation'. If you believe this sort of stuff, you're going to have a very hard time.

How about a change of belief?

Selling is about honesty; selling is about listening; selling is about helping. If you start to think of sales in this way it will be a lot easier for you. After all, don't you want to be an honest, listening, helping salesperson for your services? The good news is that excellent salespeople are exactly this way.

- **Selling as a Talent.** - You are actually a born salesperson who lost the talent as you matured. It used to be easy to ask for things and to present your case. But you became 'professional' and stopped doing what was natural. So don't worry about talent. Just learn the skills and the process.

- **Learn some basic Sales Skills** - And all the talent will come back to you naturally. What are the key sales skills? (1) Listening for what people want and need; (2) Asking questions to find out more; (3) Presenting what you have in terms of benefits; (4) Answering objections and questions with logical arguments. And finally, simply asking your prospect to take **action**. Yes, it takes time and practice to master these basic skills, but the truth is, they are at the heart of all selling.

- **How about Selling as a Process?** - For me this is the most interesting part of selling and often the most important. Selling (especially for high-end products and services) is a multi-step process that can take quite a long time. It is not a one-call proposition. So for your particular requirements you need to map out the process from A to Z before anything else. For instance, here's my sales process for selling marketing services to major prospects.

1. **Pre-qualification** - They call on me as a result of a referral or from other marketing I've done and I find out something about their needs and their situation. I tell them a little about what I do.
2. **Information** - I make sure they have enough information about me so they can at least determine if I might be able to help them or not. For this I send them a brochure or direct them to my web site.
3. **Appointment** - If I can help them and they are interested, I set up a presentation.
4. **Presentation** - I then give them a presentation to better understand where I'm coming from and so they can see the possibilities of us working together.
5. **Needs Assessment** - Next I find out everything I can about them in a face-to-face meeting to determine exactly what they need, their budget, etc.
6. **Proposal -** I write up a very specific proposal outlining exactly what objectives we will accomplish and how I will go about doing it.
7. **Negotiation** - We discuss the fine points of the proposal and come to an agreement as to how we'll proceed.
8. **Consummation** - The client signs the proposal (contract) and we start working together.

To effectively accomplish the entire process you need to be aware of what step you are on at the moment and be clear about what step you want to get to next. For the sales process to be successful, you must actively guide it; if you don't it can go in any direction. This guiding of the process is not manipulation in the traditional sense, but it is **control**. And believe it or not, prospects like to work with people who are in control, who know where they're going, who know what to do next. So yes, selling is a talent, a skill and a process. But perhaps understanding the process is the most important aspect. When you do, you are likely to close a great many more sales.

FACTUAL EXPERIENCE

Persuasion, coupled with a few of the other qualities featured in this book, came to my assistance when I lost out heavily on an abortive enterprise and had to start out all over again from scratch without discretionary funding at my command. My new venture (which I had thoroughly researched and was convinced would recoup my losses in time) had a working capital requirement of £100,000. To set the ball rolling I sold on the open market, rather than surrendered, personal insurance policies which realised £10,000. Then with a sound business plan, good judgement and gentle persuasion, I managed to negotiate an arrangement for the balance by way of a mix of public sector grants and subsidies. So far so good but to secure these grants and subsidies I had first to demonstrate my ability to obtain a bank overdraft facility, which I knew I wouldn't require to use. No bank would grant me a facility without back up collateral so I used my one and only credit card to borrow another £10,000. I received my public sector funding and opened a current account with the bank that was offering the highest interest rate on term savings accounts. Here is how I dispersed the total funding:

- I used the money borrowed on my credit card as collateral against overdraft facilities but deposited it in a high interest bearing term savings account
- I deposited the grants and subsidies funding plus my own cash in the current account- but then swiftly transferred 90 per cent to the savings account because I knew it would be some time before I would be required to use it.

Gentle persuasion got me my funding and sound judgement resulted in apportioning the cash in such a way as to pay off my credit card loan in a less punitive manner.

HELPFUL HINT

People who kick doors and shout a lot sometimes get what they want by sheer intimidation. The success is short-lived though because bullyboy tactics don't work for long. Better by far to ask for what you want through reasoned presentation and gentle persuasion. That way you won't suffer comebacks and you can also go back and ask for more without fear of downright refusal.

Chapter 18

Prepare to persist in your quest for achievement

Sometimes what we want we can't have right now because it takes time and patience to achieve. There is no way of avoiding this. Some aspirations just take longer to mature. Move on to some other goal in the meantime but never give up on your dreams. Just as William Wallace was inspired to persist as he watched a spider overcome adversity to weave its web successfully, so too must you persist in your quest for achievement.

THEY FINALLY LISTENED TO THE VOICE OF PERSISTENCE

Charles Farkas and Philippe De Backer, in their book *Maximum Leadership* (Texere Publishing 1997) relate the story of a young graduate who over forty years ago joined a Japanese company as a clerk in a small department. He applied himself faithfully to his duties but went one step further. He frequently contacted corporate headquarters to constructively highlight deficiencies in the organisation - and offered suggestions for correcting them. For ten years his ideas were rarely acknowledged and *never* acted upon.

Then one day as he was leaving work, an executive from corporate headquarters stopped him on the way out. A few minutes later he was ushered into the president's office, a place he had never even visited before. In that meeting he was informed that one of his suggestions was about to be implemented. The president expected it to save an entire division from bankruptcy. A few months later, it did just that. The story doesn't end there. The young clerk eventually became chairman of the firm that once ignored his telephone calls and memos. Because of his leadership, the culture of the organisation has been revolutionised and now individuals who challenge the status quo are encouraged, even celebrated.

The enterprising company in question is Canon - the multi-billion pound manufacturer of cameras, copiers, printers and fax machines.

PERSISTING TO ACHIEVE

Once you are clear in your own mind what it is you want to achieve, be prepared to persist until you have accomplished it. There is no point in putting thought, work and effort into developing a plan if you fail to carry it out.

The real achievers in life are not necessarily the heralded captains of industry or high profile personalities; they are those ordinary people who go about their business quietly and efficiently, ticking off each goal on the list as it is accomplished.

Plans don't just fall into line because progress never just 'happens'. You have to make it happen through persistent effort.

- **Persist in the pursuit of your goals** - Many small business owners conduct their affairs on a haphazard basis, bouncing from one crisis to another and snatching at fortune whenever they catch a fleeting glimpse of opportunity. You don't fall into this category or you would not be reading this book. You have identified your goals; prepare to persist through thick and thin until you have achieved them all.

- **Persist in all your daily undertakings** - Systematic progress in all you undertake to accomplish each working day is the cornerstone to fulfilling your ambitions in the long term. There is no other way; there are no quick fixes. Tackle your 'things-to-do' list with enthusiasm and when you have completed it, you will have taken another giant step forward.

- **Persist in developing your marketing applications** - The more curious you are about marketing techniques, the more inventive you will become in their application. Observe, study and learn the techniques with which you are not yet familiar; then put into practice those with which you feel most comfortable. That is how to test market for future achievement.

- **Persist in evolving your sales policy** - There is more than one way to sell your output, be it tangible merchandise or a personal service. Look around at how others are doing it; spend some time on the search engines identifying competitive web sites to determine whether you are perhaps lagging behind in the evolvement of your sales policy.

- **Persist in grooming your staff** - Send them on training courses or better still, conduct a seminar in your own premises. Persist in grooming them to make the best of themselves because when they do, they will bring out the best in you.

- **Persist in collecting your dues** - Never settle for customers paying you when it suits them. Persist until you fine-tune your systems to ensure that you get paid at your prescribed time, every time.

FACTUAL EXPERIENCE

I once wanted a piece of business so badly I persisted for seven years in its attainment. The product was a popular provincial newspaper, *The Glasgow Evening Times*, the stable companion of which was *The Herald*, whose marketing I had handled for several years.

Try as I might (and did) I could never get close enough to plead my case because the fact that I already had one of the publisher's products seemed to be debarring me from handling the other. Then a new editor appeared on the scene, one Charles Wilson who later became editor of *The Times*. As all new brooms should always do, Charlie called for presentations. I was invited to pitch but despite elaborate preparations, I was unsuccessful and bitterly disappointed, especially so because the account went to my nearest rival. I bit the bullet, kept my chagrin to myself, and prepared to persist. Then several months later Charlie walked into my office and asked if I would re-design the logo and masthead for his product. I did, he liked it, and then all went quiet again. Several more months later he returned again with a remit to produce a series of radio commercials. Not long after I was awarded the full-blown account after seven years of studied persistence.

Prepare to persist - and never give up - in your quest for achievement.

HELPFUL HINT

Good things can come to you through happenstance but more often than not you have to persist to achieve. When you know in your heart that what you want is right for you, persist in your endeavours even if the odds seem to be stacked against you - and never, never give up.

Chapter 19

Appreciating the awesome effect of humility

In aspiring to be an effective leader who attracts quality people, the key is to become a person of quality. Leadership is the ability to attract followers to the gifts, skills, and opportunities you offer as a business owner. And because leadership is one of the great challenges of life, it is vital that you devote time and energy to developing your skills. Great leaders keep working on themselves until they become super efficient.

These skills are all based on qualities you already possess, so there is nothing new to learn; just to refine and develop.

SKILLS BASED ON QUALITIES YOU ALREADY POSSESS

- **Inner strength**
- **Innate kindness**
- **Boldness**
- **Pride**
- **Humour**
- **Realism**
- **Humility**

And the greatest of these is humility. Great leaders always exude a pronounced sense of humility in their dealings with fellow human beings. They can be tough but never rough, gentle but never soft. The effects of genuine humility are awesome and have the power to inspire loyalty in others.

- **Learn to be strong but not rude** - It is an essential step you must take to become a powerful, capable leader with a wide ranging 'reach'. Some people mistake rudeness for strength. It's not even close to being a good substitute.

- **Learn to be kind but not weak** - You must never mistake kindness for weakness. Kindness isn't weak. Kindness is a special type of strength. You must be kind enough to tell somebody the truth. You must be kind enough and considerate enough to lay it on the line. You must be kind enough to tell it like it is and not deal in delusion.

- **Learn to be bold but not a bully** - It takes boldness to win the day. To build your influence, you've got to walk the talk in front of your group. You've got to be willing to take the first arrow, tackle the first problem, and discover the first sign of trouble.

- **Be proud but not arrogant** - It takes pride to win the day. It takes pride to build your ambition. It takes pride in community. It takes pride in cause, in accomplishment. But the key to becoming a good leader is being proud without being arrogant. In fact the worst kind of arrogance is arrogance from ignorance. It's when you don't know that you don't know. Now that kind of arrogance is intolerable. If someone is smart and arrogant, we can tolerate that up to a point. But if someone is ignorant and arrogant, that's just too much to take.

- **Develop humor without folly -** This is important for a leader. In leadership, we learn that it's okay to be witty, but not silly. It's okay to be fun, but not foolish.

- **Deal in reality** - Save yourself the agony. Just accept life as it is. Life is unique. Some people call it tragic, but in fact it's unique. The whole drama of life is unique. It's fascinating. Skills that work well for one leader may not work at all for another but the fundamental skills of leadership can be *adapted* to work well for just about everyone: at work, in the community, and at home.

- **Finally: learn to be humble, but never timid.** You can't get to the high life by being timid. Some people mistake timidity for humility. Humility is almost a God-like word. A sense of awe. A sense of wonder. An awareness of the human soul and spirit. An understanding that there is something unique about the human drama versus the rest of life. Expressed another way, humility is a grasp of the distance between the stars, and yet giving out the feeling that we're part of the stars. Humility is a virtue; but timidity is a disease.

FACTUAL EXPERIENCE

I experienced the power of humility for myself when I owned a disparate marketing services agency specialising in retailing. At the time I had only three clients, the biggest of which was a Scandinavian concern. My contact was a brash senior marketing executive of the old school who had *commanded* me to arrange a profile on the company with a leading UK national newspaper. Though never an easy assignment to see through to fulfilment, I managed to interest the Daily Telegraph in the project. Unaccountably, the executive failed to show on the day of the interview, and I was obliged to make do with his deputy. Nevertheless, when the article appeared some weeks later, I was well pleased with the result; pleased that is until I received an irate telephone call from the no-show castigating me for allowing the interview to proceed without his authority. He ended the conversation by advising me of his intent to terminate my contract. Although deeply aggrieved over the unfairness of his appraisal, I decided to write off the business and concentrate on developing the bits and pieces that represented the remainder of my clientele.

Several weeks later the deputy, who was equally upset over the impasse, called to ask if I would be agreeable to meet with his immediate superior in an endeavour to reach a compromise. I accepted his invitation.

At the meeting I was subjected to further offensive ranting until I called time on the fiasco. I proceeded to advise the executive that while I accepted that my actions had caused him distress, I had done him no harm and that it would be in the best interests of his company and mine if we sever relations immediately.

He had been expecting a fight and so establish quantifiable grounds for dismissal, but he also knew he was in the wrong. My agency held on to the account for another seven years, six of which were after he was summarily dismissed for yet another bout of arrogant behaviour towards his own immediate superior.

HELPFUL HINT

You'll meet many high hats in business circles who despise humility because they regard it as weakness. Humility is never weak; it is a spiritual quality that everyone possesses if only they knew it, and knew how to use it. Humility is strong, compassionate, understanding, and the essential quality anyone aspiring to leadership must develop.

Chapter 20

How to handle unreliable people

Surround yourself with competent, reliable people and you will ease considerably the strain of minding your business. Allow unreliable people to go anywhere near your business and they will screw it up for you. On that you can depend. I could close this chapter right now because that just about sums it up, but perhaps we ought to examine the subject in a little more detail because unreliability is sometimes difficult to detect. Difficult in that it is not necessarily systematic; it is often sporadic. Bur sporadic unreliability is enough to blow it all for you, permanently.

To err is human, to forgive is divine, but to condone unreliability is suicidal.

WHY IT ALWAYS PAYS TO INSIST ON TOTAL RELIABILITY

No one can run a business efficiently if they associate with people who are less than 100 per cent reliable; whether within or without the organisation. People who always do what they say they will do are more precious than a vault full of jewels; you'll get a higher return out of them. Unreliable people on the other hand are not only worthless; they're also a menace because you have no way of knowing when their fecklessness is going to strike out at you next. There is no set pattern; it just happens, leaving you to pick up the pieces.

Reliability from within

Not only does it afford you peace of mind; it also presents you with a few added bonuses.

- **You don't have to worry when you're out and about** - You cannot always be at the helm; be it in the office or at the factory bench. Frequently you have to flee the crow's nest to service a customer's requirements or source new business. When you are surrounded by reliability, it's comforting to know that you have left the tiller behind in safe hands.

- **You can confidently promote from existing resources** - It is always a safer bet to promote from within because you are aware of the potential you are jacking up to handle more complex assignments.

- **You can rely on reliable people to alert you to danger signals** - As your enterprise grows it becomes more and more difficult to keep a finger on the pulse of every aspect of the business. Reliable people will alert you to problems; unreliable people won't bother.

Reliability from without

You must equally be able to rely on the promises of both your customers and your suppliers. A customer who commits to a deal to accept produce or a service from you over an agreed period and who then cuts out of the arrangement without notice is a customer who is not worth having. If they do it once, they'll do it again. As to supply sources, regardless of the quantities involved, always build in a penalty clause on contracts to provide goods or service on the prescribed date. If they don't like that, find yourself another supplier.

WHY YOU MUST NEVER CONDONE UNRELIABILTY

When you allow a member of staff, a customer or a supplier to get away with even one single act of unreliability, you are opening the doors to a major disaster descending upon you when you least expect it. Refuse to accept any less than 100 per cent reliability in all of your undertakings.

FACTUAL EXPERIENCE

There was once a young lady in my employ who reminded me of Topsy in the nursery rhyme: when she was good she was very good but when she was bad she was appalling.

Although competent and attentive for most of the time, occasionally she would funk out on concentration and drop the ball with the most disastrous consequences.

I had just flown into Gatwick one Sunday evening when I noticed her staring out of a window in the passenger observation lounge. One look at her face and I knew there was trouble 'brewing' back at the ranch. She gave me the bad news.

Earlier in the week she had attended a meeting at the regional offices of Bass Charrington Breweries where she had been instructed to place on the client's behalf an important advertisement in a series of national dailies. The content was strictly hush-hush along the lines of, 'All enquiries will be treated in strictest confidence'. Unfortunately, she had been out on the town the night before the morning when she set about processing the copy, which she did with a head so thick it failed to pick up on the catastrophe she was creating. When the ads appeared a few days later they had the client's logo emblazoned across the top. In one fell swoop, one young lady's intemperance and crass unreliability had blown the client's credibility, and mine.

We lost the account but I forgave her. Bad mistake; sporadic unreliability caught up with her again some months later in similar circumstances and all but cost me another valuable piece of business. This time I dismissed her.

HELPFUL HINT

Have no truck with unreliable people either in your business or your personal life. They'll suck you dry, spit you out, and move on to cause havoc elsewhere. Grade people carefully before you hand out responsibility. If you don't, you'll be placing your very security in the safekeeping of an unknown factor.

Chapter 21

How to react to pressurised situations

As we go about our business day in day out, situations arise to put pressure on us. We cannot eliminate pressure altogether but we can minimise it if we go about matters in the right way; pressure that remains unchecked builds up quickly and drains away vital energy that would be better deployed on the more constructive aspects of everyday affairs.

WE ALL GET THE SAME 24 HOURS A DAY

How we use the hours of the working day greatly impacts upon how we react to potential pressure, and so how we set about prioritising tasks and addressing interruptions is essential work.

- **Identify and take responsibility for time-management** - It's your business and your day, so manage your time to your own best advantage.

- **Fend off casual, drop-in visitors** - If they have nothing of importance to contribute, just tell them to go away.

- **Maximise workspace through better organisation** - The working environment ought to be more than ever-increasing corners of clutter. Sort it out and help cut down on needless pressure.

- **Set time limits for projects and meetings** - Projects that take too long to complete and meetings that go on for too long invariably do so because set time limits were not imposed. Make sure everyone knows the cut-off point.

- **Prevent phone calls and emails from taking over the day** - Instigate strict disciplines, starting with you.

- **Plan for the unexpected, while building in enough time for projects** - Contingency is the key to avoiding unnecessary pressure. Always have something in reserve to legislate for the unexpected.

- **Set goals and prioritise daily tasks** - Get it all down in writing

- **Break down tasks into smaller segments** - Do it this way and delegation becomes easier.

ADDRESSING THE 'It's Needed Yesterday' SYNDROME

Everyone wants what they want and they want it now, if not sooner. It usually happens first thing on Monday morning or very late on Friday afternoon; Monday because they couldn't be bothered on Friday; Friday because they have other fish to fry on Monday. While it may be an admirable trait to attempt to cater for everyone's needs all of the time, it is rarely profitable.

- **Target your efforts on the most important tasks** - You know what needs doing now. Refuse to be deflected.

- **Be a goal-getter, not just a goal setter** - You set the targets, make certain you achieve them.

- **Do the most constructive thing first to make life easier later** - The first task on your list might well be the nastiest but it will also turn out to be the most constructive if you get it out of the way first.

- **Avoid time-wasters** - They just hold you back from where you want to be arriving: mission accomplished.

- **Use the R-A-F-T theory to attack those dreaded stacks of paper** - Read and assess; file or trash. If it's worth keeping, keep it. If it's not, bin it.

- **Delegate, delegate, delegate** - You'll get there all the quicker if you do.

STAUNCHING PRESSURE BEFORE IT REACHES BOILING POINT

No matter how well organised you are, sometimes something comes at you out of the blue to catch you unawares and create pressure. It doesn't have to be a crisis; just some matter sufficiently vexatious as to warrant your immediate attention. Such unexpected happenings can have an unsettling effect, knocking you off your stride unless remedial action is undertaken at the outset.

Identify the issue, isolate it, and address its resolution before the pressure builds up to reach boiling point.

FACTUAL EXPERIENCE

I was once the co-vendor in the sale of a business where my minimal shareholding netted me an unusually high return; unusually high because I had played hard-to-get in the negotiations for disposal. Several months later the purchasers belatedly discovered anomalies in the stated trading returns and demanded their money back. Their main target was the other vendor against whom they instigated court proceedings. They couldn't take me to court because they hadn't actually paid me a brass farthing; the consideration for my shares having come from the proceeds of the sale via the other vendor under a separate arrangement. Instead the purchasers came after me directly for the return of that which they considered to be rightfully theirs.

The pressure was incessant and not a day passed without demands and veiled threats of reprisal. I was in the clear legally but because I still had to do business with my oppressors, something had to done to resolve the impasse.

I had three choices.

- I could pay them back in full
- I could tough it out
- I could negotiate a middle way

As always when facing difficult decisions I turned the problem over to my subconscious. Catharsis and osmosis took over, aided and abetted by intuition (see Chapter 25).

Here is what I did.

I offered to *lend* the purchasers a sum of money equating what I had received from the deal but on condition that it be used to relieve the indebtedness of the ailing concern they had just taken over. I set a time limit of two years for the loan to be repaid in full by the holding company plus compounding interest at 2 per cent above the base bank lending rate.

They did not like the terms of my offer but they accepted them.

As it happened, I was reimbursed with interest within six months because wiser heads than theirs prevailed against allowing the arrangement to run its prescribed course.

HELPFUL HINT

A certain degree of pressure in handling everyday affairs is inevitable and indeed can prove beneficial when the effects are channelled correctly. Restrict the tension in your life to an acceptable level by fending off people and situations that cause unnecessary pressure.

Chapter 22

How to cope with treachery

Treach•er•y, [n]:
1. Willful betrayal of fidelity, confidence, or trust;
2. The act or an instance of such betrayal.

Treachery creeps up on you like a thief in the night. It doesn't make appointments nor does it leave a calling card; it just strikes at the core of your being and your business. Acts of treachery can occur at any time within your own ranks, with a customer, a supplier or a competitor.

It is well said that, *'By seeing your defenses through the eyes of your worst enemy, you become your best guardian.'*

TREACHERY WITHIN YOUR OWN RANKS

Employees can betray your trust in ways that are not easy to detect. They could be gossiping out of office hours about sensitive matters germane to the security of your business. They could be surreptitiously stealing from you and not necessarily cash or merchandise; your very livelihood could be the target.

TREACHERY FROM A CUSTOMER

How could a customer commit an act of treachery against you? Easy; you wouldn't be the first to have invested time and money in preparing expensive confidential specifications only to have them passed over to a competitor with a view to inveigling the receiver of your intellectual property into providing the treacherous customer with the prescribed goods or service at cheaper rates.

TREACHERY FROM A SUPPLIER

The majority of supply providers are trustworthy and respectful of sensitive customer intelligence imparted to them in the line of duty. However, you might have the misfortune to stray into the path of an unscrupulous merchant who would use the information for spurious purposes and leave you hanging out to dry in the process.

TREACHERY FROM A COMPETITOR

We all have a living to make and most of us conduct our affairs with integrity, but whatever line of business you operate, beware the fly-by-night competitor who would commit an act of betrayal against your reputation without flinching.

COPING WITH ACTS OF BETRAYAL

When you are the victim of a treacherous act it is only natural to want to lash out and exact vengeance, but fighting treachery with treachery is counter productive. This is not to imply that you should do nothing. On the contrary, what you should be doing is taking stock and devising ways to exact not vengeance but retribution appropriate to the offence.

When a member of staff betrays you - In the event of substantiated malicious gossip or rumour mongering, present your evidence, enact a notice of dismissal and provide the offender with an unhelpful reference on the way out. If someone is stealing from you in cash or kind (no matter how insignificant the amounts), call in the police immediately. If it is part of your business that has been stolen, go out of your way to make it extremely difficult for the thief to make capital out of the unethically acquired opportunity.

When a customer betrays you - Irrespective of the value of the contribution to turnover, close the account immediately. You should not be doing business with anyone who betrays a confidence. Get up, go out and acquire some new business to compensate for the temporary loss.

When a supplier betrays you - Shop them to the appropriate trade association. Genuine supply sources will applaud your condemnation of the offender.

When a competitor betrays you - Spread details of the chicanery among your customers and colleagues in the trade. Then put the boot in by contacting the trade press.

None of these are acts of vengeance; they are acts of retribution. The subtle distinction makes all the difference but the effect is just as punitive…

FACTUAL EXPERIENCE

I once had a bright young man working in one of my enterprises, so bright I edged him along to maturity by systematically delegating his way more and more complex assignments. Eventually I elevated him to director status. One day he came into my office and informed me that he was leaving to set up on his own account. He proceeded to demonstrate that the format of his enterprise would in no way cut across or impose a threat to my business. He was totally open and forthright and even requested that I accompany him to visit premises on which he had a tentative lock on the lease. I did so and suggested some minor improvements he might undertake to achieve a more productive working environment. At the eleventh hour when I had all but sealed the deal on his replacement, he recanted and asked if he could stay on as he had decided he wasn't ready yet to take the leap into self-employment. I agreed, and that is where I went wrong. I had failed to observe the warning signals that this young man was as tricky as he was undoubtedly bright. I should have imposed a minimum time limit on his renewed stay of tenure.

Nine months down the line when sales were going through the roof, I returned from a business trip to discover that my prodigy had flown the nest without warning, taking with him three of my upper-income bracket clients; the practice was too well rounded and financially sound to be seriously threatened by this aggregated defection, but I felt betrayed. I wanted retribution and I exacted it. What the defectors had failed to take into consideration was that my enterprise operated under the auspices of a powerful trade association that placed a requirement on departing clients to settle their outstanding commitments in full before they could deal through another source.

The combined dues amounted to in excess of £250,000 and while the money was safe and I would have been paid eventually, I insisted on immediate remittance. My act of retribution softened the cough of my ex-employee, set his start-up back before it got off the launching pad, and caused a flurry among the financial directors of the defecting clientele.

The young man's business nose-dived within a year but I was not the architect of his downfall; he managed that all by himself.

HELPFUL HINT

Treachery is an insidious act and those who inflict its perfidious consequences on others are to be avoided like the plague. When you first detect treachery in your affairs, enact the appropriate strategy for retribution, and then cut off all routes for its re-occurrence.

Chapter 23

Facing up to the fear factor

"Through the gateway of feeling your fear lies your security and safety"
—Unknown Author

Fear of any description is an erosive emotion and if we allow it to insinuate its way into everyday business affairs it can quickly turn into anxiety, minor depression, or even a crisis. No one is immune to the fear factor and no one should treat the matter lightly. There is however a positive side to fear and when we learn how to handle it, we can turn the fear factor to advantage and strengthen our resolve. Feeling the fear is to examine cause and overcome effect.

THE POSITIVE SIDE OF FEAR

You can be concerned yet unafraid and that is the positive side of fear but left to its own devices, even the slightest fear can start pressing alarm bells and invite panic to take over. Identify your fears as they occur; look them straight in the eye and analyse them. They will relate to one of two things; that which you can do something about, that which you can do nothing about. If you can handle it, fix it by doing something, *anything* to put matters right. If it is outwith your control, forget it.

Permitting concern to develop into fear is utterly destructive. It has a damaging effect on health and stability, and presents an even greater threat to your business operations than any of the conventional concerns that you can and should be addressing.

SOME MATTERS OF CONCERN FOR SMALL BUSINESS OPERATORS

- ***Concern over the future*** - *'What if there is a change in consumer preferences and people stop using my product/service?'*; *'What if the industry becomes obsolete?'* There are only two things certain about life: (1) one day you are born; (2) one day you will die. The bit in between is what you make of it. Time spent on speculating about future happenings is time wasted. Remember the old adage, 'Today is the tomorrow that you spent your time worrying about yesterday.' Take each day as it comes and plan as best you can for tomorrow.

- ***Concern over health matters*** - *'I worry about falling into ill health. I'd have to close my business'*. When you are working for yourself, such concerns are as real as they are understandable. But worrying about them won't help because worry in itself is a disease; keep busy, keep active, keep up your fitness levels, and you will contribute greatly to your own sustained wellbeing. If concern over health matters remains an issue, invest in some appropriate insurance cover for the self-employed.

- ***Concern over money*** - *'What if I run out of money and can't pay my bills?'* Look after your cash flow on a daily basis (Chapters 4 and 30) and when you spot the odd distress signal, take remedial action. Conversely, if the worst happens as it has to some (myself included) and you were to lose all your money, then acquire some more capital and start all over again. Money is only a commodity, the loss of which can always be replaced. Lose an arm or a leg, and it's gone forever.

- ***Concern over decision making*** - *'I dread making decisions because I'm always afraid I'll make the wrong one'*. For some this is a problem and it shouldn't be; we all make the odd bad decision and usually because we're not thinking straight at the time. If decision making is a concern for you, go back and read Chapter 12

- ***Concern over competition*** - *'I worry about what the shop down the road will get up to next; price cutting, special offers, they're always up to something'*. Comfort yourself with the knowledge that if there was no competition around, there might not be *any* custom coming your way. Observe competitive activity by all means but never worry about it. Leave them to worry about what you get up to.

- ***Concern over failure*** - *'I'm in constant fear of failure, I couldn't bear the shame'* There is no failure in a business going under and neither is there any shame attached. In any case, you cannot fail unless you give up completely (Chapter 10).

ADDRESSING PROBLEMATIC SITUATIONS AS THEY OCCUR

The very beginnings of fear arise when you are suddenly confronted with a problematic situation, the resolution to which you have no easy answer. There is an immediate temptation to blank out the problem by shoving it to the back of your mind. That certainly eliminates the fear factor temporarily but unless you first *consciously* address your problematic situation, the fear factor will soon return to haunt you. Examine it, warts and all, then commit it to the subconscious and your precious innate gift of intuition (Chapter 25) will provide you with the answer.

HOW TO HANDLE THE FEAR FACTOR

In most cases the only thing we have to fear is fear itself because we are frequently uncertain as to exactly what it is we're concerned about, when it started and how it was triggered off. That's why introspection is essential.

- **Face up to it** - Grab the fear factor by the scruff of its hypothetical neck and ask what it's doing in your life. Dissect it.

- **Talk to someone** - Choose someone you can trust and share your feelings. More often than not that does the trick because you will probably find that he/she has had a similar experience and can be of genuine assistance.

- **Look at yourself** - Do you have a propensity to worry over minor matters? Is the cup always half-empty? Work on it.

FACTUAL EXPERIENCE

Not once but twice in my life I have been in the grip of fear over businesses that were struggling and running out of control, and twice I came out of it by talking to wiser heads than mine. One of these enterprises survived and went on to prosper; the other did not. But neither outcome was as significant as the knowledge I acquired on how to handle the fear factor.

This double jeopardy scenario occurred during the early part of my career and since then I have never been fearful of *anything* in business - and I do mean anything.

HELPFUL HINT

There are truthfully very few hurdles you will encounter in your journey of entrepreneurship that you cannot overcome somehow or other. When a molehill looks like a mountain, just feel the fear. Relax, analyse the problem, discard the impossible and get on with that which can be done.

Chapter 24

How to manage in a crisis

" **Crisis** *n*. a crucial or decisive moment; a turning point; a time of difficulty or distress; an emergency"

Note: crucial, decisive, emergency. Your business is motoring along successfully when suddenly something happens to turn everything on its head, the very thing you least expected. That's what a crisis is; something nasty arriving on your doorstep without prior warning. After the initial shock, you are faced with two options:

(1) Panic, freeze, do nothing, and watch the crisis intensify;

(2) Feel the fear, reflect, and start thinking positively.

Feeling the fear is good because it galvanises you into action, positive action that prompts you to tackle the crisis with the as much energy as you would apply if it were an opportunity you were handling.

Now, if the crisis warranted it and your business could bear the cost, you could call in one of those ever-multiplying crisis management consultancies. Choose this path and you will be presented with a formula for management (accompanied by a high priced ticket for accomplishment) that would look something like this:

- Identify the crisis
- Isolate the crisis
- Manage the crisis

- Crisis communications
- Media relations
- Damage control
- Assemble a crisis management team
- Create a crisis management plan
- Crisis forecasting
- Crisis intervention
- Decision making under crisis-induced stress

Yours is a small business that can ill-afford to hire a consultant who might well resolve the crisis but perhaps drive you to the brink of bankruptcy in the process. So, what to do?

Take the formula and do it yourself. It's your business, your future, and your crisis.

- **Identify the crisis** - If you haven't cottoned on yet, you are not paying attention. What exactly is it? How serious is it? Make a list of the repercussions it could have on your business. How did it come about? Who, if anyone, is to blame? Could it re-occur? Could it have a bounce-on effect on other aspects of the business? Does it warrant calling in expert assistance? These are the sort of questions you'll want to address before you do anything in the way of effecting resolution or taking remedial action.

- **Isolate the crisis** - Treat it as a separate issue, removing it from everyday activity in order to avoid its effects spreading to other areas of the enterprise.

- **Manage the crisis** - Tackle it head on. Do something, anything, at the outset to obviate further damage.

Assume immediate responsibility for creating a plan of action.

- **Crisis communications** - Treat communications on a strictly need-to-know basis. In other words, don't run around the workplace like a headless chicken spreading alarm and despondency. Confide only in those who can be of genuine assistance.

- **Media relations** - As it is highly unlikely that your little business is about to invaded by news hounds from the press and broadcast media, stay tight and handle with aplomb any enquiries that might arise. Do not though go into denial - or hand the matter over to a public relations consultant unless events prove to be beyond your capabilities.

- **Damage control** - Bite the bullet and assess just how much damage has been done to date, how much more could occur. Devise your own damage limitation strategy.

- **Assemble a crisis management team** - If you are a one-man operation, your team is already in position. If you have partners or senior executives, get them involved on addressing specific aspects of the crisis.

- **Create a crisis management plan** - Now take out your A4 pad, draw a line down the middle, and start formulating your overall plan of recovery.

- **Crisis forecasting** - What's the very worst that could happen? Write it down. What eventual outcome might you be prepared to settle for? Write it down.

- **Crisis intervention** - Are there any external parties affected by the crisis who might want to get involved? Determine whether their intervention would be a help or a hindrance.

- **Decision making under crisis-induced stress** - There is no way around this. You have to stay calm and in control no matter how stressed out you may feel. The best anyone can accomplish in a crucial situation is to do his/her very best to find a way out of it.

EXAMPLES OF CRISES THAT CAN STRIKE ANY BUSINESS AT ANY TIME

There are dozens of disparate scenarios for crisis descending on a business and they all strike like thieves in the night. Here are a few of the most common.

- Cash suddenly running out because of inefficient accounting control
- Essential supply sources drying up unexpectedly due to closure, bankruptcy, liquidation or receivership
- Walk-outs or strike action by employees
- Major customer abruptly ceasing to trade with you
- Customer litigation against the company on a grand scale

- Writ issued against the company on unpaid dues when there are insufficient funds available to meet the demand
- Loss of business occasioned by defection of senior executive(s)
- Serious production error that places the business in jeopardy

You can add to these flood, fire and malicious damage, which although covered by insurance can frequently have crucial effects on a small business.

FACTUAL EXPERIENCE

At around five o'clock in the evening I returned to the office feeling well pleased. I had been meeting with the Scottish Development Agency who confirmed that my marketing services operation had been awarded their image account for Japan. This win, on top of the accounts we already held for the United Kingdom, Europe and the USA, meant that we were now handling all of their business.

The door opened to admit my two fellow directors who were evidencing looks of utter dejection. 'We have a major crisis on our hands,' said one of them. Major crisis was an understatement. It was a mega-crisis with awesome implications regarding tenure of the accounts we had so painstakingly nurtured to date.

That very morning the first insertion of a series of full-page advertisements in the SDAs initial North American campaign had appeared in eight major daily newspapers spread across the USA from eastern to western seaboards. In these ads a New York telephone number was prominently featured. It was the number to call for high level contact on enquiries relating to inward investment.

But it was the wrong number.

Had it been a non-number, things wouldn't have looked quite so black. But it was a real telephone number, that of a Chinese Takeaway in Lower Manhattan. Having been bombarded with a series of inexplicable calls that morning, the owner had contacted his local PSB (public service broadcasting) station whose controller had some fun on air over the fiasco and then contacted the Wall Street Journal. This was the first of the newspapers to break that day carrying the gaff and it was this journal that had brought the matter to the attention of my co-directors.

While it was all a big hoot in New York, it was no laughing matter back home.

The client was as yet unaware of the problem (or they'd have let us know by now in no uncertain terms) and to compound the agony, there was another insertion due in a few days time in all eight newspapers. Fortunately, they all had New York representation.

Quickly I got to the root of the disaster. Several months beforehand and before the actual telephone number was available, a layout artist had concocted his own (prophetic) series of digits for the purposes of a presentation rough. Incredibly, this Mickey Mouse telephone number had gone all the way through the system undetected to final artwork which even more incredibly the client had approved. The client's complicity though was of no comfort. The crisis had to be addressed and addressed straightaway.

I telephoned the client before close of play, admitted all, and gave notice of what I intended to do. Here is what I did.

- I personally amended the artwork for all eight publications because at the time
- I trusted no one else to do it.
- I caught a flight next morning for New York.
- I tendered my abject apologies to the SDA American representative that evening.
- Next morning I did the rounds of all eight publications providing them with fresh artwork for subsequent insertions.
- Finally, I called in on the bewildered takeaway owner to express my regrets over the inconvenience occasioned him.

During my brief trip I was the butt of many jibes and when I returned back home there was no brass band, no plaudits - only an eerie silence from my employees and the client.

All I had really accomplished with my swashbuckling approach to the crisis was to effect damage limitation and secure a stay of execution. The rot had set in though and eighteen months later when it was official government review time, we had used up all our brownie points and the account moved on.

On the other hand, had it been a commercial concern I had offended by this act of idiocy, I would have been fired instantly - and rightly so.

HELPFUL HINT

When the roof falls in, take a ten-second break for despair and then crack on formulating a plan of recovery. Crisis management doesn't call for any special skills; only the application of common sense and sound judgement. Isolate the crisis and then resolve it by accomplishing each step in the formula detailed in this chapter.

Chapter 25

Cultivate intuition by listening to the inner voice

Intuition is becoming increasingly recognised by psychologists as a natural mental faculty, a key element in the creative process, a means of discovery, problem solving, and decision making. Once considered the province of a gifted few, it is now recognised as an innate capacity available to everyone--not a rare, accidental talent, but a natural skill anyone can cultivate. A key ingredient in what we call genius, it is also an important tool when applied to everyday business affairs.

It is an incredible weapon to have at your command in an arsenal of strategy making techniques, but it doesn't just happen and you cannot switch on at will until you first learn how to cultivate intuition by listening to the inner voice that resides within you.

There are several excellent books on the subject that you can purchase at good bookstores or perhaps borrow from your local central public library but here are some basic pointers to help you get started on your quest to reach the inner voice.

SLOWING DOWN AND LISTENING TO THE INNER VOICE

Information is proliferating at such a frenzied rate today that even with personal computers and cellular phones (*or perhaps because of them*) your attention is stretched to the extreme. Not only do you have more facts about more diverse fields of information than ever before, you are also subject to a greater array of outcries and opinions.

Fortunately, beneath all the cacophony of the information age, the quiet truth about problem solving, decision making, and opportunity seeking in business is always available to you. By learning to slow down and pay attention to **what's right under your nose,** you have a chance to find your own authentic answers, unaided by media and technology. To do that you must build up your 'intuition muscle' and learn to centre yourself in the present moment. It's only at your core, in the here-and-now eye of the global information hurricane, that you can hear the inner voice.

HOW ATTUNED ARE YOU TO THE SUBTLE MESSAGES AROUND YOU?

Messages like those hidden behind your spoken communication.

There is guidance available to you at all times, just below the surface of logic, just **after** you stop pushing and striving, just **before** you jump to conclusions. By cultivating the ability to pause and be comfortable with silence, and then by focusing steadily and listening for the first sounds or feeling for the first impressions, you can help your intuition wake up suddenly and enthusiastically, as if from a long winter's nap.

In my own searching to cultivate the inner voice, I've learned to listen for the faintest of whispers, the nearly silent song. One of the most important skills in developing accurate intuition is the ability to tone down your domineering talk-addicted mind, which arrogantly thinks it knows how the world works without ever observing what's happening in the freshly occurring present moment. To know clearly, you must learn to observe neutrally, and true observation can only take place with a silent mind.

SOFTEN YOUR AWARENESS

Activating intuition always starts with a down gear shift into softness and silence. You'll never receive accurate information with a chattering mind, clenched as tight as a fist. Recall how you feel when you're concentrating on meeting a deadline and worrying about doing a good job in the time frame. Your brow is furrowed, you're shackled to the task in hand, and you're probably way ahead of yourself, anxious to achieve the intended goal. This is your 'masculine mind' in operation; the kind of awareness men and women alike must use to achieve concrete results. You are in your linear, left-brained masculine mind so often, you've come to identify it as normal and you tend to forget that there is an equally powerful, complementary state of consciousness that is quiet, unhurried, highly creative and tension-free: the 'feminine mind', the right hand side of your brain.

The feminine mind is not goal-oriented; it simply observes, includes, appreciates, and is present in whatever it notices.

TRY THIS SIMPLE EXERCISE

Every day regardless of what's happening around me, the strife, demands on my time or whatever, I take ten minutes out to reach the inner voice, and here is how I do it.

Firstly, I cut off all communication.

Then I lean back in my chair, put my hands flat out on the desk, empty my mind and enter a state of self-induced but *controlled* hypnosis. I instruct my subconscious to awake me in exactly ten minutes, count down from ten to one, and switch off completely.

Right on cue ten minutes later, I come out of my reverie and count up from one to ten. I open my eyes and awake to a cleansed mind, disengaged from useless paraphernalia and brimful of new thoughts, ideas, and solutions to problems unresolved.

Think I'm crazy?

Try it. You'll be amazed at the results you'll receive in clarification and purification of your innate mental prowess. This technique is particularly useful when faced with a vexatious problem or a tricky situation that calls for a calculated decision.

Intuition provides the answers when the subjective mind can not.

Stick with this exercise every day for a few months and soon your intuition will begin to work automatically during waking hours, providing you at will with a steady stream of new ideas and solutions.

FACTUAL EXPERIENCE

I related earlier how abject carelessness cost my consultancy the Scottish Development Agency accounts. Now let me tell you how intuition played a vital part in getting a finger into the business in the first place.

Some six months after its formation this central government quango (popularly known as the SDA) issued an invitation to a select number of concerns to present proposals for the Agency's first ever promotional campaign covering the United Kingdom. We were numbered among the select few and I was elated.

My co-directors, however, did not share my enthusiasm. They were of the opinion that our consultancy was insufficiently geared up to handle such a high profile public sector operation. I disagreed on two counts (1) there was no profile as yet, and (2) I had worked previously with the chairman and several of the senior executives, and was confident that we could quickly strike up a working chemistry with the various divisions we would be representing.

When the brief arrived, my colleagues were even less convinced. It was brevity personified, consisting solely of three short, well-couched paragraphs.

I locked myself away in my office, read the brief several more times, switched off and tuned into the silent mind. When I awoke, two words were firmly implanted on my consciousness, 'awareness' and 'property'.

I reflected for a few moments on the revelation and then returned to the brief. Buried in the text under highfalutin terminology were indirect references to 'awareness' and 'property', promotion of which I perceived to be the core requirement of the exercise.

'Awareness' inasmuch as the SDA had no image awareness at all as yet and 'property' because the client was the landlord of hundreds of public sector commercial and industrial properties which were all crying out for promotion.

'Awareness' and 'property' were the twin platforms we used in our presentation for the business, which we won - and then (as previously documented) subsequently lost for the most absurd of reasons.

HELPFUL HINT

Intuition is a free gift provided by nature to assist *anyone* who takes the trouble to master the simple technique of contact with the inner voice that resides within everyone. Practise the technique daily and soon you will be able to reach your innate intuitive resources at.

Chapter 26

Learning to ask for what you want

The old adage - *If You Don't Ask, You Don't Get* - is also a truism, and yet some people balk at the prospect of asking someone else for what they want. No one is going to hand you a million pounds just for the asking but, if it's within their orbit of expertise, they might show you how to set about earning that amount of money for yourself. Information is the commodity that business people want; they want to know how to do this, that and the other, and if they don't ask around, they miss out.

They miss out because what they want is freely available if only they would take the trouble to ask. Only the twisted and bitter will refuse a reasonable request for information which is within their domain to impart.

WHO CAN YOU ASK FOR WHAT YOU WANT?

You can ask whom you like, providing it's someone with the wherewithal or the power to provide you with what you are seeking. I once wrote to Tony Blair asking what he thought about the concept of a book I was about to write, *Selling to the Public Sector*, How To Books 2000. By return I received a reply from one of his aides stating that the Prime Minister thought it was a good idea and a worthwhile project.

Now, I wasn't asking for the PMs permission to *write* the book because I didn't need his approval to proceed. What I wanted was to create awareness at the highest level in the public sector that such a book was in the melting pot, and I succeeded. I got exactly what I wanted with the proviso that I didn't use the 'endorsement' for promotional purposes. That was not an issue because I had already indicated in my request that such was not my intention.

Ask at the very the very pinnacle of the information tree wherever you can

It is always a good policy to go straight to the top in your quest for what you want, especially when dealing with institutions. While it is not always possible, try it wherever you can because you will knock out the middleman and anyone else empowered to block your progress.

At the time of the last reorganisation of local government I was in urgent need of a list of contact reference points for all the newly appointed marketing officers in hundreds of newly restructured councils. There was nothing written down because reference manuals had yet to be published. I decided to go straight to the top and drafted a request to the chief executive of every new council in the form of an official questionnaire (public sector CEOs love filling in questionnaires or having someone else do it for them). The results were astonishing. I had a 98 per cent strike rate with responses pouring in daily on an exercise, which by any other means would have taken me months to complete, if at all.

- **Never be afraid to go straight to the top** - Most supremos got where they are today by asking the right questions yesterday. Moreover, they frequently have a statutory obligation to respond - even some of those operating in the private sector.

Ask around friends, relatives and colleagues

Most of the people you know are walking wells of expert knowledge on some topic or other. So next time you are stumped for an answer, look around your circle of friends, relatives and colleagues and determine whether any of them might know something about what you want to know. If you strike lucky, they will open up and give you what you want because people everywhere just love mouthing off on their own expertise.

- **Never brood over what you don't yet know** - Just ask and the chances are you will get what you want.

HOW DO YOU GO ABOUT ASKING?

For instant results it is best practice to be direct and ask face-to-face. When this is not an option you could…

- **Write a letter** - but make it interesting and novel (like including a carefully couched questionnaire, for example).
- **Send an email** - submitted along the same lines.
- **Make a telephone call** - but if it's to someone you don't know, think twice before you do. With a direct vocal approach minus the benefit of eye-to-eye contact, strangers will often suspect your motives. That said, it worked for me once, as you will shortly learn.

When you have asked for what you want...
If you get a result, send a thank-you note. If you don't, try again, but don't pester. It's just possible that the information you have requested is considered to be of a sensitive nature by the source concerned.

WHEN DID YOU LAST ASK YOUR EMPLOYEES FOR INFORMATION?

Your employees are another excellent avenue of valuable information. In any case you should be asking them frequently how they are, do they enjoy what they do, and do they have any suggestions to offer on improvements. Bin the 'suggs' box and ask them outright. A friend of mine in the consumer electronics industry once asked a junior for his opinion on a certain type of factory application. After some persuasion the boy opened up and advised my friend that he thought it was rubbish and then proceeded to outline a much more productive alternative. It was adopted painlessly and saved the company thousands of pounds on annual production costs.

Promising employees frequently move on because management never takes the trouble to ask them for an opinion. Try asking your staff for information now and again. Serendipity might step in with a surprising bonus.

COULD YOU INCLUDE A WIN-WIN BONUS IN YOUR REQUEST?

When asking for what you want is by way of a favour, try including in the request a bonus for the other party. Something along the lines of, 'If you do this for me, I'll do that for you.' This is a particularly useful strategy when dealing with people or entities unknown to you.

FACTUAL EXPERIENCE

Back in 1969 when my first marketing agency was four months old, my number one client who operated a chain of electrical stores asked me to dream up an idea for a spring promotion, but not just any old promotion, a super duper promotion. Working on a limited budget, my partner suggested a holiday for two for three weeks at the world famous Calgary Stampede. So 'Stampede!' was to be our theme, we called the client straightaway, he liked it, and we were in business. Minutes later he called back with a request: how were we planning to launch the promotion?

That evening I was sitting at home glancing through the evening paper when my eye fell upon a picture of the movie star Betty Grable sitting on the stoop of the American Embassy in Grosvenor Square. The caption read, 'Betty Grable arrives in London to start rehearsals on a new stage musical *Belle Starr*. Before opening at the Aldwych in late summer, the show will have a provincial run starting at the Alhambra Theatre in Glasgow on Monday 14 April'.

The date was perfect. It coincided exactly with the launch of our 'Stampede!' promotion and the correlation of the themes was equally perfect. I telephoned my partner, advised him of my discovery and commented what a pity it was we couldn't cash in.

'What do you mean 'a pity'? Let's go for it,' he replied.

Next morning, Saturday, we met at the office and he made the first move. He called the American Embassy and because he was young, fearless, and could walk through brick walls unscathed, asked straight out if they could provide a London telephone number for Betty Grable. Not only did he get it, he also got Ginger Rogers' number for good measure. (Such a thing could never happen now in these days of ultra high security).

Now it was my turn. I dialed the number, a voice answered, and it was that of another film star, Rory Calhoun, who it later transpired was one of the show's backers. I briefly outlined the purpose of my call,

'I'd like to secure the services of Betty Grable and the cast on arrival in Glasgow to travel the short distance from the airport to the Alhambra Theatre in a covered wagon'

There was a pause and then he replied,

'Okay, sounds good, meet up with us at 2pm on Monday at our rehearsal rooms, The Welsh Institute in Grays Inn Road'

I did, they listened, approved the scheme, and Calhoun asked,

'What's the tab?'

Now, I wasn't looking for a fee from them; I intended to pay for the service. So we split the difference and everyone got a win-win bonus. I still treasure the black and white press pics with my then four-year old daughter presenting the delightful Betty Grable with a bouquet of flowers on arrival at the airport.

All this plus the advertising and PR accounts for the show's provincial run - and all because we simply asked for what we wanted.

HELPFUL HINT

You should never be afraid to ask for what you want providing that (1) you know exactly **what** it is you are seeking, and (2) you know **how** to ask for it. Never go without when you can have what you need by simply **asking** for it in the right way.

Chapter 27

Ensuring a return on loyalty

When we show loyalty to other people we have a right to expect a commensurate return; from customers and suppliers, and most especially from our employees; conversely, when other people put their trust in us we have a duty to reward their loyalty; win-win. But loyalty has become a dubious buzzword in recent years, bandied about by marketing gurus in a proliferation of formats for customer loyalty programmes; do these work and are they all they are cracked up to be?

MYTHS ABOUT CUSTOMER LOYALTY PROGRAMMES

Building customer loyalty makes good commercial sense but as with most aspects of highfalutin marketing, there are certain myths surrounding the ethos of the sculptured and much vaunted programme approach. Here are a few.

Loyalty Myth 1:

Loyalty Rewards Programmes Prevent Customer Defections

You can't apply a loyalty reward 'sticking plaster' to a customer defection problem that is in need of stitches. No matter how good the loyalty currency, it cannot make up for deficient produce, uncompetitive pricing, or servicing problems. When customer defections are endemic, the root causes must be identified and treated accordingly. Loyalty programmes won't do it. The solution lies in asking customers what they want, listening to their feedback, and implementing solutions focused on resolving issues.

Loyalty Myth 2:

All Customers Are Equally Valuable

Some business owners mistakenly believe that all customers need to be treated with equal levels of service and attention. Yet, are all customers equal in their levels of value to the business? Are some customers unprofitable? Do they deserve the same attention as profitable customers? In the context of customer loyalty it is acceptable to play favourites, yet many designer loyalty programmes set out to provide something for everyone. The sensible loyalty reward programme should be structured to attract and motivate profitable behaviours and nothing less.

Loyalty Myth 3:

Acquiring New Business Costs More Than Retaining Existing Customers

This statement would be accurate if all customers were equally profitable but the hard fact is that not every customer is worth keeping. Some customers are worth losing to the competition if they are causing the business to lose money. Interestingly though, some operators have a hard time letting go of the revenues from under-performing customers because they fail to appreciate that revenue does not equal profit.

Successful loyalty programmes should not only be capable of retaining preferred existing customers but (when marketed to the competition's clientele) have the propensity to attract profitable customers from them as well.

Loyalty Myth 4:

Customer Loyalty & Incentives Programmes Are One And The Same

There may be similarities but they are not the same; they are representative of two different customer strategies. Incentives programmes function primarily as customer acquisition tools and are generally characterised by low award values such as small amounts of cash, coupons and merchandise. They do not have the power to drive long-term customer loyalty.

Loyalty Myth 5:

If You Reward Customers They Will Return

Oh yes? Try telling that to operators that invested sizeable chunks of money in loyalty programmes and got nothing back in return. Creating a loyalty programme is not as simple as choosing a reward and giving it to loyal customers. Most designer programmes make the mistake of failing to offer rewards that are sufficiently motivating - and then they wonder why the programme takes a nose dive.

Loyalty Myth 6:

Customer Loyalty Hinges On Strategic Marketing
No it does not. The most successful loyalty programme is the one that has highly empowered leadership from the top and is fully supported by all members of staff.

ESTABLISHING YOUR OWN CORPORATE LOYALTY PROGRAMME

You don't need a sculpted loyalty programme and you certainly do not need a marketing guru to design it for you. What we are talking about here is basic common sense, which is the essence of all true marketing initiatives.

- **Look after your customers** - Always give them your best shot but in proportion to their value to your enterprise. Cosset them if you will but never be afraid to grade them in line with profitability.

- **Look after your suppliers** - If your suppliers are providing you with consistently good service, tell them; if they are not, tell them. Building up good supply sources depends heavily on loyalty; make sure you get a fair return on yours.

- **Look after your employees** - Their loyalty is your future. People are more important than profit, so always look after your assets, but insist on 100 per cent return on loyalty extended.

FACTUAL EXPERIENCE

At a time when I numbered several divisions of Philips UK among my clientele, the managing director of one of these divisions approached me on the matter of producing some desk research and providing him with comprehensive (but speculative) marketing proposals on a new project. As he was not only a client but also my friend, I readily acceded to his request which he prevailed upon me to treat as confidential because it was just one of several tentative ventures in the melting pot. When I returned to present my offerings he and his immediate colleagues were well pleased. Next thing I knew they had all been summarily dismissed from their posts and were purported to be setting up on their own, using my proposals as one of the starting blocks.

Some weeks later my friend telephoned to ask if I would give some thought to handling the marketing requirements of his new concern on a permanent basis, but before I could give the matter *any* thought I was summonsed to a meeting with the CEO of the Philips UK holding company. Following an icy reception the CEO reluctantly around to appreciating that I had been an unwitting pawn in the subterfuge and had certainly not been privy to the conspiracy. Then he asked me outright, 'Do you intend to continue doing business with these people?' I could answer that one and I replied in the negative for two reasons: (1) I too had been deceived, and (2) his contribution to my turnover was worth a hundred times what theirs was ever likely to be.

Sometimes loyalty carries with it a price that is just too high to pay, and when that happens, you must stand aside and protect your own corner.

HELPFUL HINT

Never confuse altruism with loyalty. Altruism is a commendable quality that seeks no return for service rendered while loyalty is a two-way process that should be measured out in equal proportions. Loyalty does not exist when the shares are unequal.

Chapter 28

Protect your intellectual property or watch it vanish overnight

An intellectual property is any product of the human intellect that is unique, novel, neither overt nor obvious, and which has some **value in the marketplace**. No matter what sort of enterprise you operate, you are almost certainly the possessor of at least one intellectual property. It may be the distinctive packaging wrapped around the knobblewockers you manufacture, your unique selling proposition (USP), how you handle and resolve complaints, or even how you go about effectively collecting your dues.

Intellectual properties have no requirement for flamboyance. They can be as dull as ditch water but what they do require is the protection of their value to you in the marketplace.

TYPES OF INTELLECTUAL PROPERTIES

They come in all shapes and sizes, they can be tangible or intangible, but they have one thing in common: their uniqueness.

- **An idea**. Ideas are the lifeblood of any business but many of them float around unprotected in the turbulent seas of commercial practice. The idea that launched your enterprise is an intellectual property.

Countless others may also be using it but the version you employ carries your particular mark. Protect it.

- **Invention.** Conversely, the premise on which your business operates may be of your own devising, an invention that as such is especially vulnerable to illicit replication by others. Protect it.

- **Expression or literary creation.** It could be a book, a thesis, a poem, or an illustration, but incredibly you don't necessarily require to create this type of intellectual property all by yourself. Others may do it for you. Through popular usage, expressions such as 'I'm doing a Delia' and 'Going for a Delia' have recently found their way into Collins Concise Dictionary.

- **Unique brand name** Peter Dyson may have sold the reproduction rights of his unique vacuum cleaner but the brand name Dyson will live on in perpetuity.

- **Business method.** Could be as simple as how you market your produce, simple in your eyes perhaps but conceivably the envy of others. Protect it.

- **Industrial process.** Maybe you employ an unusual process in the production of your knobblewockers, something that the competition would love to lay their hands on. Protect it.

- **Chemical formula.** Same principle involved, same protection required. The recipe for Coca-Cola, for example, has remained a family secret for many generations.

- **Computer programme process** - Think about this: the man who invented the electronic 'mouse' does not and never will receive a penny in royalties because he failed to protect his intellectual property. It all goes to the company that employed him during the time he was developing his unique application. Countless millions use his invention every day from which he earns zilch.

- **Presentation**. How you package your produce, how you lay out your stall, how you make your sales pitch: every unique form of presentation is an intellectual property that must be preserved.

LEGAL FORMS OF PROTECTION

Copyright owners have five basic rights with regard to their work: They hold the rights for:

- Reproduction
- Distribution
- Public performance
- Public display
- Modification

WHERE PROTECTION IS UNAVAILABLE

Sadly, not every intellectual property is open to protection by legal means. Your property may be too general in nature and unique only in the sense of the twist you put on it. In such circumstances secrecy is your only recourse to protection. Tell no one about your 'twist' or you will leave yourself wide open to replication as happened to me once in the far distant reaches of time. It also happened to a company executive several years ago when in his excitement at being interviewed live on the Radio 4 *Today* programme he inadvertently let slip information relating to a secret process used by his employers in the manufacture of their produce. It came as no surprise when a competitor snapped up the details and started using the gaff to their advantage.

FACTUAL EXPERIENCE

I started my own first business at the tender age of fifteen, selling personalised festive stationery around the doors. Though cumbersome, over-alliterative and long-winded, the trading name was nonetheless snazzy: **'The Snowball Christmas Card and Calendar Company'**. Little did I realise when I tremulously set out on my first calls how prophetic was to prove the inclusion of the seasonal noun 'snowball' in the title.

You see, in those days, no one else was offering such a service in my area. It was a novelty that was not available in local shops and to locate it via mail order would have required one to dig very deeply. From day one my strike rate was inordinately high and moreover, each time I sealed a deal the snowball effect clicked into place. Not only did I pick up a sale, I was also provided with a gratuitous list of qualified prospects in the shape of friends, neighbours and relations residing in the immediate vicinity. It was like shooting fish in a barrel. And my good fortune didn't end there. Soon I was being approached by community stores to act as agents for my service and (although I did not appreciate it at the time) the magic of replication was increasing my sales and hiking up the profits.

Come the following festive season, the inevitable happened through lack of foresight. I had competition on my door-to-door calls and most of the agent shopkeepers were now operating the service on their own account.

I had learned my first lesson in minding your own business. Leave your intellectual property unprotected and it will leave you hanging out to dry on the line. What could I have done by way of protecting the idea behind my first business venture? Well, for a start, I could have resisted the temptation to hand out the freebie sales receipts provided by my supplier. They carried an ad on the reverse with his contact details…

HELPFUL HINT

It might not appear staggeringly obvious but somewhere in the philosophy of your enterprise there is an intellectual property at work. Protect it by whatever means at your disposal or risk handing it over to someone else for nix.

Chapter 29

Being in the right place at the right time

Luck is best defined as "The intersection where opportunity and preparedness meet"
(Author unknown)

Preparedness meaning that you have availed yourself of the facts and are inspired to embrace those facts and move forward. And so being in the right place at the right time is more often than not down to developing the nous to spot an opportunity and carve a niche for your particular expertise. Occasionally you might luck out and hit the big one without effort but that doesn't happen often enough to get fazed about.

The trick is to *plan* to be in the right place at the right time.

SEARCHING FOR OPPORTUNITIES WITHIN YOUR ORBIT OF EXPERIENCE

How can anyone plan ahead for opportunity? You can and you must if you wish to uncover the streams of gold that lie hidden within your own orbit of experience. It's easy to develop a mind set on whatever it is you do to make a living; to become convinced that how you currently operate is all there is to it. But there is more, there's always more if you take the trouble to dig deeply.

During World War 2 my Uncle Jim ran a general food store situated in the middle of a vast sprawling housing estate on the outskirts of a seaside village. The market was there in abundance right on his doorstep but he became increasing frustrated at his inability to service it due to rationing and the national scarcity of staple foodstuffs.

One afternoon as he was leaning on a rail at the shore-side he watched the local fishermen hauling in their catch for the day. The idea came to him; he would sell fish and chips from opening to closing time in his general store. Now he had no idea how the business worked but as he had been retailing all his life he reckoned it couldn't be too difficult. He made some enquiries regarding equipment and supply sources, and (perhaps because he was a local councillor) managed to obtain the necessary planning permission. Within weeks his new sub-enterprise was launched and proved so popular that he purchased additional premises at either end of the long street in the middle of which his food store was situated. He opened them as fully-fledged fish restaurants. Seven decades on and all three outlets are still trading.

CARVING A NICHE BY MATCHING OPPORTUNITY TO EXPERTISE

Being in the right place at the right time invariably emanates from coupling *perceived* opportunity with acquired expertise. When Sir Alan Sugar first set up in business it was as a manufacturer of domestic electronic entertainment appliances but he soon found that it was virtually impossible to compete with low cost, low price foreign imports. Unlike many long established competitors who succumbed and went under, he set about turning competitive superiority to his own advantage. He took them on at their own game by importing the components in kit form and distributing the assembled merchandise under the now famous Amstrad brand.

Look too at how the major supermarkets milk being in the right place at the right time. Whoever thought you could arrange your banking, mortgage, and insurance requirements through the local grocer?

Being in the right place at the right time when you know what you're getting into

The safest route to diversification is to spread your wings within your own orbit of experience; it's the safest because you always know what you getting into. Examine your options to diversify in this way, plan ahead, and create a new profit centre - or two.

Being in the right place at the right time as a specialist

When you are particularly good at what you do, you become acknowledged as a specialist in your sector. Spread the word near and far about your expertise and more often then not, you will find yourself in the right place at the right time.

Being in the right place at the right time anywhere in the world

In Chapter 1 we discussed how broadening your horizons generates new ideas. Now let us examine the proposition from another angle. Unless your enterprise is *strictly* localised in nature, and regardless of whether you operate from a thatched cottage in Nairn or a converted loft in Potters Bar, you can reach out and be in the right place at the right time doing business with anyone, anywhere in the world.

FACTUAL EXPERIENCE

I've had several books published over the years, some of which have been in style for a while then disappeared, others have bombed, but two of these titles just keep going on from strength to strength. Why? Why should two out of several prove so popular? They are popular because they are directed at niche markets that are self-perpetuating and have a seemingly bottomless pit of prospective participants. Like the London Buses, there's always another one coming along in a minute.

Back in 1994 when I wrote *Starting Your Own Business* (How To Books), government initiatives on helping people to start up on their own were just beginning to bite. As these initiatives increased in volume, so too did interest in my work. Similarly, when I became increasingly aware of the hype on home based web operations, I wrote *Starting an Internet Business at Home* (Kogan Page). This latter tome has only been around since August 2000 but it is already selling well in bookstores all over the world and (as I suspected it would) as an Internet download via Amazon, BOL, Barnes & Noble, etc.

Now, spotting an opportunity and carving a niche for yourself only works when you know the market inside out and when it identifies *precisely* with your own expertise. Look again at the marketplace in which you operate and establish whether there is a sector or sub-sector that is tailor made for exploitation through your special brand of knowledge. That is how to position yourself in the right place at the right time.

It has nothing to do with luck; the answer lies in creative thinking followed by entrepreneurial flair.

HELPFUL HINT

"The intersection where opportunity and preparedness meet" translates into recognising fortunate happenstance and making the most of it through appropriate planning. In other words, make your own luck out of every opportunity that comes along.

Chapter 30

Strategies for efficient cash flow management

We have touched on the subject of cash flow several times in this book. Now let's look at the subject in greater depth because no matter what else you may get wrong in your affairs, this is the one area you must *always* get right.

SOLVING CASH FLOW PROBLEMS

If any single term can define what it is that makes or breaks a business, it must surely be cash flow. Even if you have the best staff, customers, suppliers and ideas, with a bad cash flow situation your business is likely to go bankrupt rather quickly. For our purposes, we will work with cash flow in its simplest form; the principle that a company's income should be the same as, if not higher than, its expenditures. Sounds simple. So why do so many businesses get it wrong?

Keeping your cash flow in good order

Whether chronic or temporary, cash flow problems could mark the end of your business. If you can't pay off a debt in the extended time allowed but you know you're going to receive £20,000 the week after, this still might not be enough. Let's go over a few general strategies to keeping your cash flow in order:

- **Hire a good accountant** - Whether you have a professional person working on your books or just your Auntie Maggie preparing the figures to pass on to an auditor, make sure they're good at their job. If your business has more than a couple of employees, the benefits of hiring a good accountant should more than outweigh the cost. He/she will also be more qualified to give you advice on tax loopholes and ways to avoid future cash flow problems.

- **Be diplomatic and don't lie** - If you can be diplomatic with your customers and those who *you* owe money to, you are half way there to solving your cash flow problems. Be honest with people you owe money to. If you can't pay back an installment on a loan within the time required, negotiate a deal and show them that you're definitely going to have money available to pay the installment at a later date. Most creditors will support you if you're honest with them. After all, it's not in their interests for you to go bankrupt and be unable to pay off the debt.

- **Cutting down on expenses** - If you can cut down your expenditures just by a little each month, you can save up money to prevent future cash flow problems. Even if you are flush with cash in one month it doesn't mean you will be the next. Try not to work on the brink of insolvency all the time.

- **Keeping abreast with your financial situation** - Keeping the books balanced isn't as easy as it initially seems. Even if you have a great accountant, it's important that you yourself keep abreast with your financial situation. Even more important is that you rationally deal with bad cash flow situations and invest your money wisely when your cash flow situation is good.

What if though you have to dig deeper because cash control is becoming a chronic problem? No matter what you try, the cash flow dilemma keeps recurring. When this happens your options (if any) are very limited.

Why redundancy isn't a quick fix for chronic cash flow problems

Laying off, redundancies, voluntary leave, call them what you will, they all involve getting rid of people from a business to reduce costs. However, if you run a small operation, making people redundant is a false economy. You might save several hundred or several thousand a month, but didn't you hire the people in the first place to help you make more money? In large concerns, the laws of efficiency state that there are a certain percentage of workers that aren't contributing to the company's profits, and that these people can be removed without too much hassle. In a small business, however, there are *less* people and so each person probably has a bigger role to play in generating revenue for the company. The best advice is not to look at redundancies as being the quick fix for chronic cash flow problems, but to look at it as a **last resort**.

Of course, if you want to get rid of staff but retain their revenue generating abilities, there's another option available to you, rehire them as freelancers.

Rehiring staff on a freelance basis
If you want to make some of your people redundant but feel guilty about letting trusted workers down, you could rehire them as freelancers. Many businesses are taking this option, especially in the media and entertainment industries. Moreover, because freelancers work from home, they may feel more comfortable and perhaps produce more output for you. Not only that: they will be able to obtain work from other sources to boost income. Freelancing is normally beneficial to everyone involved.

But if cutting down on staff costs isn't going to solve your problems, what can you do to raise some more significant funds?

Selling a share of the business privately
If your enterprise isn't big enough to go public or if you don't wish to be put under intense scrutiny, consider privately selling a share of your business instead; this is a process where you sell a percentage of your company to someone for a fixed sum of money. If you totally own the company, then this money is technically *yours* but you can choose to invest it straight back into your business. Alternatively, you could keep the money and save the company money by reducing your wage to zero.

The problem with selling a share of your company privately is finding a buyer. Any interested party is going to want to see your accounts and might not be keen if they see your cash flow is in a bad way. Accordingly, people who are friends or family (because they will be more likely to trust you) usually take up this option.

Alternatively, if you can find a like minded professional with an interest in your business, consider selling a share. It can bring your business new optimism and hope, as well as much needed money.

FACTUAL EXPERIENCE

I have already confessed to you that I am mathematically challenged but regardless of my innate deficiency, I have always endeavoured to maintain sound cash control in all of my enterprises. Having a reliable accountant at my elbow is essential, but however *you* go about matters, make sure that you are comfortable with your cash flow at all times.

Your living and your peace of mind depend upon it.

Good luck, and may the wind of fortune be always at your back…

HELPFUL HINT

You can be the master of every other strategy in this book and still come a cropper if you fail to manage your cash efficiently. Look after the cash flow every day of your working life.

Chapter 31

Monitoring growth using an audit checklist

Sometimes a small business fails because the owner is unaware of the many elements that can prevent the operation from growing and becoming successful, and this because the business is organised around the manager's specific area of expertise, such as marketing, accounting or production. Such specialised expertise often prevents the owner from recognising problems that may arise in other areas of the enterprise. This chapter provides the small business entrepreneur with the essentials for conducting a comprehensive search to locate existing or potential problems and for addressing opportunities as they arise

This instrument is not exhaustive i.e. the reader must rely on personal judgment and previous experience. However, it does provide a systematic framework to ensure that critical areas have been addressed before action is taken. The audit is a tool, not a replacement for good management skills. Audits cannot do your job. However, effectively designed instruments such as this audit can save valuable time for the seasoned professional as well as the novice small business manager.

HOW TO USE THE AUDIT FOR MAXIMUM EFFECTIVENESS

- **Answer all questions** with an affirmative indicating no problem or a negative indicating the presence of a problem in a specific area.
- **Review the analysis** of each section of the audit to determine what action is most appropriate.

THE AUDIT ANALYSIS

The audit analysis focuses on a variety of elements under seven critical business functions: *basic planning, general bookkeeping and accounting practices, financial planning, sales and marketing, advertising and promotion, personnel and production* - and these functions under three major audits: the **management** audit, the **operations** audit and the **financial** audit. In the healthy and financially sound small business, these seven functional areas are in balance. However, the reader cannot work on all seven areas of the audit at once; you must decide on which areas to concentrate, based on past practices and the needs of your enterprise. Regular use of this audit instrument will help to make you more efficient in managing your business affairs.

Audit Checklist for Growing Businesses

THE MANAGEMENT AUDIT

- Basic Planning
- Personnel

THE OPERATIONS AUDIT

- Production
- Sales and marketing
- Advertising and promotion

THE FINANCIAL AUDIT

- General bookkeeping and accounting practices
- Financial planning and loan proposals

THE MANAGEMENT AUDIT
Yes No

I. Basic Planning

A. The business has a clearly defined mission. ____ ____

    1. There is a written mission statement. ____ ____

    2. The business is carrying out the mission. ____ ____

    3. Mission statement is modified when necessary.

    ____ ____

    4. Employees understand and share in the mission.

    ____ ____

B. The business has a written sales plan. ____ ____

    1. Market niche has been identified. ____ ____

2. New product lines are developed when appropriate.
   _____ _____

3. Targeted customers are being reached. _____ _____

4. Sales are increasing. _____ _____

C. The business has an annual budget. _____ _____

   1. Budget is used as a flexible guide. _____ _____

   2. Budget is used as a control device. _____ _____

   3. Actual expenditures are compared against budgeted expenditures. _____ _____

   4. Corrective action is taken when expenses are over budget. _____ _____

   5. Owner prepares budget. _____ _____

   6. The budget is realistic. _____ _____

D. The business has a pricing policy. _____ _____

   1. Products or services are competitively priced.
      _____ _____

   2. Business provides volume discounts. _____ _____

   3. Prices are increased when warranted. _____ _____

4. There is a relationship between pricing changes and sales volume. ____ ____

5. New prices are placed on last-in goods when the price on old stock gets changed. ____ ____

II. Personnel

A. Employees know what is expected of them. ____ ____

1. Each employee has only one supervisor. ____ ____

2. Supervisors have authority commensurate with responsibility. ____ ____

3. Employees volunteer critical information to their supervisor. ____ ____

4. Employees are using their skills on the job. ____ ____

5. Employees feel adequately trained. ____ ____

B. Each employee has a job description. ____ ____

1. Employees can accurately describe what they do. ____ ____

2. Employecs do what is expected of them. ____ ____

3. Workload is distributed equitably. ____ ____

4. Employees receive feedback on performance. ____ ____

5. Employees are rewarded for good performance. ____ ____

6. Employees are familiar with company policies. ____ ____

7. There is a concise policy manual. ____ ____

C. Preventive discipline is used when appropriate. ____ ____

1. Employees are informed when performance is below standard. ____ ____

2. Unexcused absences are dealt with immediately. ____ ____

3. Theft prevention measures are in place. ____ ____

D. Regular employee meetings are conducted. ____ ____

1. Employees' ideas are solicited at meetings. ____ ____

2. An agenda is given to employees prior to the meeting. ____ ____

THE OPERATIONS AUDIT

                                                                          Yes No

I. Production

A. The business has a good relationship with suppliers.

                                                                         ____ ____

1. A well-documented plan addresses how to deal with suppliers. ____ ____

2. Inventory delivery times are specified. ____ ____

3. Levels of quality of materials and services are specified. ____ ____

4. Payment terms are documented. ____ ____

5. Contingency plans are provided. ____ ____

6. Regular contact is made with suppliers. ____ ____

B. The business provides for good inventory control.

                                                                          ____ ____

1. Business has an inventory control formula to provide for optimum inventory levels. ____ ____

2. Business has a policy on securing inventory in a timely fashion. ____ ____

C. The business conducts incoming inventory inspections. _____ _____

   1. There is a written policy on incoming inspection. _____ _____

   2. Incoming inspection is being performed. _____ _____

   3. Incoming inspection levels of quality are documented. _____ _____

D. The business has alternate sources of raw materials. _____ _____

   1. Two or more suppliers are identified for each product required. _____ _____

   2. The majority of raw material requirements are divided equally between two major suppliers with a third source receiving lesser value but consistent orders. _____ _____

E. The business has a routine maintenance programme. _____ _____

   1. A routine maintenance programme is documented and communicated to all maintenance personnel. _____ _____

   2. Every major piece of equipment has a maintenance log positioned in an obvious place. _____ _____

3. Preventive maintenance is a regular occurrence.

F. **The business has a formal operator-training programme.**

   1. Business has a written operator training manual.

   2. A progressive training process is in place.

   3. Accomplished operators are identified to answer questions from trainees.

   4. Constructive feedback on training progress is provided in a non-intimidating fashion.

G. **The business meets Health and Safety Executive (HSE) standards.**

   1. The business is aware of HSE standards pertaining to the nature of the enterprise.

   2. The business conducts regular meetings with employees concerning HSE standards.

   3. All safety records and lost time accidents are documented.

H. **The business has a well-documented processing procedure.**

1. A scheduling process enables orders to be grouped for more efficient processing. ____ ____

2. A scheduling chart allowing instantaneous recognition of production status is positioned in an obvious place. ____ ____

3. Sub-assemblies are manufactured in sufficient quantities on a timely basis. ____ ____

4. Finished stock is safely transported to a clean and dry area. ____ ____

5. Adequate controls are provided to preclude excessive
inventory buildups that could result in finished
stock spoilage or obsolescence. ____ ____

I. The business has an environmental awareness policy. ____ ____

1. A policy pertaining to the disposition of hazardous waste materials is fully documented and communicated to all relevant parties. ____ ____

2. Attempts are made to stay current with all existing regulations pertaining to the environment. ____ ____

3. Regular meetings are conducted to determine better methods of dealing with by-products. ____ ____

J. The business keeps up to date with technological advances. ____ ____

    1. Company representatives attend trade shows on a regular basis. ____ ____

    2. Business subscribes to trade publications. ____ ____

    3. A formal employee suggestion programme is in place. ____ ____

    4. Business conducts regular technology advancement brainstorming sessions involving the employees. ____ ____

    5. Business is involved in community extended learning programmes. ____ ____

II. Sales and Marketing

A. The owner knows exactly what the business is. ____ ____

    1. The owner knows exactly who the customer is. ____ ____

    2. Potential customers know about the business. ____ ____

    3. Location is appropriate for the business. ____ ____

    4. The market is clearly defined. ____ ____

B. The owner knows competitors and their location. _____ _____

1. The owner knows how his or her prices compare with those of the competition. _____ _____

2. The owner knows how the competition is regarded. _____ _____

3. Census data are used for strategic marketing. _____ _____

4. The owner is aware of regional sales patterns. _____ _____

C. The owner and employees focus on customer needs. _____ _____

1. The owner and employees treat customers courteously. _____ _____

2. Customer concerns, complaints and suggestions are listened to carefully. _____ _____

3. Customers are provided with quick, reliable service. _____ _____

4. Customers consider the owner knowledgeable. _____ _____

5. Appropriate housekeeping procedures for the business are rigidly pursued. _____ _____

D. The owner is aware of customer needs. ___ ___

    1. Feedback is requested from customers. ___ ___

    2. Sales receipts are monitored. ___ ___

    3. Sales receipts are compared to those from previous years. ___ ___

    4. Seasonal variations are taken into account.

    ___ ___

E. The business needs to increase sales volume.

    ___ ___

    1. There is a sales plan in effect. ___ ___

    2. Sales targets are being met. ___ ___

    3. Effective sales presentations are being made to potential customers on a regular basis. ___ ___

    4. Names of prospects are kept in a follow-up file.

    ___ ___

    5. Sales are closed effectively. ___ ___

III. Advertising and Promotion

A. The owner has an advertising and promotional plan.

    ___ ___

1. Has an advertising budget. ____ ____
2. Advertises monthly. ____ ____
3. Advertises weekly. ____ ____
4. Has a promotional calendar. ____ ____

B. The owner uses effective advertising and promotion.
____ ____

1. Advertises in Yellow Pages. ____ ____
2. Uses conventional newspapers and free sheets. ____ ____
3. Uses radio and television advertising. ____ ____
4. Obtains no-cost or low-cost media coverage. ____ ____

C. The owner uses effective merchandising techniques.
____ ____

1. Relates display space to sales potential. ____ ____
2. Uses vendor promotional aids. ____ ____
3. Knows traffic flow patterns of customers. ____ ____
4. Ensures that all facilities are clean. ____ ____

D. The owner evaluates advertising and promotional efforts. ___ ___

  1. Determines if sales increase with advertising. ___ ___

  2. Ascertains if sales increase after special promotions. ___ ___

  3. Ascertains whether advertising is reaching intended market. ___ ___

THE FINANCIAL AUDIT

Yes No

I. General Bookkeeping and Accounting Practices

A. The company has a bookkeeping system. ___

single entry _____
double entry _____

The owner

1. Prepares the books. ___ ___

  a. Understands the how and why. ___ ___

  b. Prepares own financial statements. ___ ___

2. Pays for bookkeeping service. ___ ___

    a. Understands financial statements. ___ ___

    b. Has taxes done by bookkeeper. ___ ___

    c. Has compared cost for bookkeeper with that of a certified accountant. ___ ___

B. The business reconciles bank statements monthly. ___ ___

C. The business keeps income and expense statements accurate and prepares statements monthly. ___ ___

The owner

    1. Understands the purpose of financial statements. ___ ___

    2. Compares several monthly statements for trends. ___ ___

    3. Compares statements against industry averages. ___ ___

    4. Knows current financial status of business. ___ ___

D. The business makes provision for VAT. ___ ___

The owner

    1. Understands the procedures. ____ ____

    2. Makes payment on time to avoid penalties.
        ____ ____

    3. Provides all relevant information. ____ ____

E. The business has a credit policy. ____ ____

    1. Ages billing system monthly. ____ ____

    2. Accesses late payment fee from customers. ____ ____

    3. Writes off bad debts. ____ ____

    4. Has good collection policies. ____ ____

    5. Has a series of increasingly pointed letters to collect from late customers. ____ ____

    6. Has VISA, MasterCard, or other credit card system.
        ____ ____

    7. Offers discounts for early payment. ____ ____

F. The company files all tax returns in a timely manner. ____ ____

The owner

    1. Considers tax implications of equipment early. ___ ___

    2. Considers buy versus lease possibilities. ___ ___

II. Financial Planning and Loan Proposals

A. The business has an adequate cash flow. ___ ___

    1. Cash receipts are monitored and accounted for. ___ ___

    2. Cheques are deposited properly each day. ___ ___

    3. Customer invoicing is done promptly (within two working days). ___ ___

    4. Collections are received within 30 days. ___ ___

    5. Accounts payable takes advantage of cash discounts. ___ ___

    6. Disbursements are made to best effect. ___ ___

B. The business projects cash-flow needs. ___ ___

    1. Payrolls are met without problems. ___ ___

    2. Money is set aside for expansion, emergencies and opportune purchases. ___ ___

    3. Short-term financing is used when needed.

       ___ ___

    4. Line of credit is established with a bank. ___ ___

C. The business understands the role of financial planning in today's highly competitive lending markets. ___ ___

    1. The owner's personal resume is up to date.

       ___ ___

    2. Personal financial statements have been prepared.

       ___ ___

    3. The business has a written business plan. ___ ___

    4. Source and use of funds statements exist for the past two years, with a projection for the next two years.

       ___ ___

    5. An accurate balance sheet exists for the past two years and includes a projection for the next two years.

       ___ ___

6. The owner has a good working relationship with the bank. ____ ____

7. There is a strong debt-to-equity ratio. ____ ____

Complete an initial audit and you will readily appreciate why the seven critical business functions - *basic planning, general bookkeeping and accounting practices, financial planning and loan proposals, sales and marketing, advertising and promotion, personnel and production* - dovetail and interrelate - and why it is vital for the growth of your enterprise that you undertake these audits on a regular basis.

While this particular model for an audit checklist has a strong manufacturing bias, you may alter, edit or completely re-structure the format to meet with your own specific requirements.

Epilogue

All of the strategies featured in this book are tried, tested and proven. Apply them in your daily undertakings and your business will prosper. In the event that one (or more) of the ten deadly mistakes that can bring down an enterprise currently plagues you, refer to the following listing for precise chapter targeting on your particular problem(s).

Getting wedded to an idea and sticking with it for too long

    Chapter 1
    Chapter 25
    Chapter 29

Operating without a viable marketing plan
    Chapter 2
    Chapter 11
    Chapter 14
    Chapter 15
    Chapter 17
    Chapter 28

Failing to appreciate market forces
    Chapter 3
    Chapter 13

Ignoring your cash position
   Chapter 4
   Chapter 30

Ignoring employees
   Chapter 5
   Chapter 20
   Chapter 27

Confusing likelihood with reality
   Chapter 6
   Chapter 13
   Chapter 19

Operating without a sales strategy
   Chapter 7
   Chapter 26
   Chapter 29

Playing the Lone Ranger with no back up
   Chapter 5
   Chapter 8
   Chapter 16

Operating with no mastermind on board
   Chapter 8
   Chapter 9
   Chapter 13

Giving up
   Chapter 10
   Chapter 11

Chapter 12
Chapter 13
Chapter 18
Chapter 21
Chapter 22
Chapter 23
Chapter 24

Glossary of Business Terms

Analysis paralysis. The situation arising when a problematic situation is over-analysed, resulting in confusion and subsequent frustration.

Buying patterns. The methodology used by customers (wholesale, retail and end) in choosing merchandise for purchase.

Buying policy. The criteria set out for purchasing raw materials for manufacture or produce for re-sale.

Cash flow. The essential ingredient for success in any form or trading; cash flow is the difference between cash coming into a business and cash flowing out.

Centering. Used in this context as the ability to apply single-minded focus on any given situation.

Channel of information. Cyberspace terminology that highlights the facility for using the Internet as a device for receiving and delivering information.

Collecting dues. Collecting the cash due on commercial transactions.

Consumer preference. The criteria exercised in selecting merchandise for purchase.

Dedicated search engine. The introduction of a search engine dedicated to assisting visitors to access aggregated page content in a web site.

Deliverable information. Information available for transmission from one web site to another.

Distribution policy. The routes chosen for the distribution of a product or service.

Downloadable product or service. Any commodity capable of conversion into an electronic format that can subsequently be downloaded on the Internet..

E-service. Using the Internet as a dedicated vehicle for the provision of customer service.

Ezine. An electronic newsletter distributed via the Internet.

Feminine mind. The right side of the brain; specialising in the creative process.

Footfall. Store traffic.

Guest book: An electronic device that allows web site visitors to register personal details.

Information tree. Used in this context as a compendium of sources for requesting information.

Intuition. That part of the mind that when successfully accessed provides answers and solutions.

Left hand brain. The side of the brain that handles the practicalities of life.

Masculine mind. Alternative name for the left brain.

Master plan. Personally devised overall strategy for success in business.

Mission statement. The summary of a master plan.

Non-cash items. Those commitments in the accounts of a business that have been invoiced in but not yet paid out.

Order button. Device on a web site allowing for the electronic ordering of produce.

Payment terms. Defined stipulation for settlement of outstanding accounts.

Paypoint or Payzone facility. Alternative commercial facilities that enable retailers to earn commissions and increase footfall by accepting payment for designated consumer utility accounts.

Premium. The offer a free product with the purchase of dedicated merchandise.

Receivable information. Information capable of receipt or download from one web site to another.

Right hand brain. The side of the brain that provides the creative process.

Sales machine. The process that determines how, where, when, and from whom sales emanate in business transactions.

Selling policy. The prescribed factors that govern the sales process.

Strategy. Plan for fulfilment.

The 80/20 rule. More of a theory than a defined rule, which estimates that 80 per cent of the content in any given web site appeals to only 20 per cent of the cyberspace audience.

The R-A-F-T theory. Read and assess; file or trash.